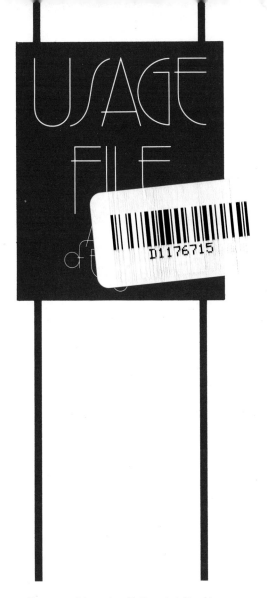

USAGE FILE

D1176715

Prepared by the Editorial Staff

SCOTT, FORESMAN AND COMPANY

Design / Bronwyn Rex

USAGE FILE American of English

CONTENTS:

FILE DRAWER 3

FILE DRAWER 4

FILE DRAWER 5

FILE DRAWER 6

AMERICAN

ENGLISH USAGE

...the whys & wherefores

There are in the world some 300 million people whose native language is English. Yet, as you have certainly observed, they do not all speak exactly the same kind of English. For instance, there are some very obvious differences between the British brand of English and the American (U.S.) brand.

When you watch a British movie, does it sometimes take you a minute or two to get your ear tuned to British pronunciation? It does most Americans. For one thing, the British tend to speak more rapidly than we and to swallow letters and slur syllables (like the *sary* and *tary* of *necessary* and *secretary*). They stress words differently too. For example, we stress the *lab* in *laboratory*; the British stress the *bor*. We usually stress the *cier* of *financier*; the British stress the *nan*. We say *specialty* and stress the first syllable; the British say *speciality* (with a second *i*) and stress the *al*.

The British also give a different value to some vowels. The next time you hear someone from England speaking in a movie or on TV (David Frost would be good), pay attention to his pronunciation of words like *ask*, *rather*, *not*, *sport*, and *phone*; you will probably find that he pronounces the *a*'s and *o*'s slightly differently from you. You may also hear him pronounce the word *clerk* as though it were spelled *clark*, *lieutenant* as though it began with *lef* (*leftenant*), and *schedule* with a /sh/ not a /sk/ sound at the beginning.

In reading books and magazines published in Britain, you have probably noticed some other differences. The British spell words like *labor*, *color*, and *splendor* with an *-our* ending (*labour*, *colour*, *splendour*). They put an *-re* ending on words like *center*, *meter*, and *somber* (*centre*, *metre*, *sombre*). Where we use a *ct* in words like *reflection* and *connection*, a *z* in words like *apologize* and *civilize*, and an *s* in words like *defense* and *pretense*, the British use an *x*, an *s*, and a *c* (*reflexion*, *connexion*, *apologise*, *civilise*, *defence*, *pretence*). They double letters that we do not, like the *g* in *wagon* (*waggon*), the *l* in *traveler* (*traveller*), and the *s* in *focused* (*focussed*). And the British spelling of some words like *jail* (*gaol*), *curb* (*kerb*), *check* (*cheque*), *tire* (*tyre*), and *program* (*programme*) differs considerably from ours.

3

The greatest difference, however, is probably in vocabulary. An American driving a car in Britain soon learns, for instance, that a no-passing zone is indicated by a sign saying NO OVERTAKING. The sign BENDS indicates that there are sharp curves ahead; NO STOPPING ON THE VERGE means "no parking on the shoulder"; and DIVERSION AHEAD signals a detour, not entertainment.

Here are some other examples of vocabulary differences:

BRITISH	AMERICAN
petrol	gas
lorry	truck
[medical] certificate	prescription
biscuits	crackers or cookies
multiple shop	chain store
vegetable marrow	squash
trunk call	long-distance call
kiosk	newsstand
goods waggon	freight car
dust bin	garbage can
single ticket	one-way ticket
return ticket	round-trip ticket
public school	private school
council school	public school
suspenders	garters
braces	suspenders
caravan	trailer
tube	subway
draughts	checkers

In addition, there are some differences in idiom. In Britain you might get a job waiting *at* table; in America you would wait *on* table. In Britain you might hear someone ask, "Will you get *off* with that excuse?" In America the question would be, "Will you get *by* with that excuse?" A British family lives *in* Green Street; an American family lives *on* Green Street.

The British also sometimes drop the noun marker *the* in a spot where Americans would use it, or they use *the* where Americans generally use *a* or *an*. In Britain, for example, someone is said to be *in hospital*; in America we say someone is *in* **the** *hospital*. In Britain a price might be quoted as "seventy pence *the* bushel." An American would ordinarily say "two dollars *a* bushel."

Some "Americanisms" amuse the British, just as some "Briticisms" amuse Americans. But differences in vocabulary and idiom can occasionally be more confusing than amusing. During World War II the United States Army Quartermasters Corps had to compile an American-British vocabulary list for its men stationed in Britain, to prevent orders for supplies from being delayed or misfilled because British suppliers were not familiar with or had other meanings for certain American terms.

Mario Pei, who has written a number of books on language, tells a story about the confusion once caused by Briticisms. Immediately after the opening of one of his shows in London, an American theatrical producer received a cable from his British agent. The cable read: "Show a success; am posting notices." In American theatrical shoptalk *posting notices* means "announcing that the show is closing." Naturally the horrified producer immediately cabled back, demanding to know why, if the show was a success, it was being closed. A return cable put his mind at ease. The agent had not been using theatrical shoptalk; he merely meant that he was mailing (posting) the critical reviews (notices). Unfortunately for the producer, he had put his message in "British."

But the differences between American and British English do not end here. What we have been considering is just one kind of British English. If you were to spend some time traveling around Britain, you would soon discover that the British do not all speak alike. This fact was pointed up not long ago by Alistair Cooke, when he was introducing a TV play based on Stella Gibbons's novel *Cold Comfort Farm*. Mr. Cooke ended his introduction with the remark that American viewers would probably have difficulty understanding some of the characters in the play, since they were using the kind of English spoken in rural Sussex, a county in southeastern England. "But," he added comfortingly, "don't let it bother you; many British viewers didn't understand them either."

The same thing would probably have happened if the play had been set in some of the other counties in England — Yorkshire, say, or Lincolnshire or Somerset — or in parts of Scotland or Ireland. Though Britain is small, the varieties of English there are numerous.

Why is this? Well, before there were trains and planes and cars, the people in different areas of Britain did not come in contact with each other very much. Gradually the speech of the people living in one area of the country acquired certain characteristics — of pronunciation, vocabulary, and so on — that made it different from the speech of people in other areas. Or to put it in a linguist's terms, each area acquired its own *dialect*.

Though there were, and still are, considerable differences between some of these British *regional dialects*, the differences never became so great as to prevent communication. They might slow it down, however, as in the case of the TV play.

Eventually such dialectal differences will probably disappear. One reason is that, thanks to the invention of the train, the plane, and the automobile, British people no longer live in isolated groups. They are continually traveling to other areas of Britain, meeting people from other areas, working with people from other areas. They read the same books, newspapers, and magazines; see the same advertising; use the same products. And the more they communicate and intermingle — the more they have in common — the more similar their speech becomes.

Still another reason is that British people today are getting more schooling. In school they become familiar with the language of educated people, which generally avoids regionalisms. Radio and TV have also had a considerable influence on British people's speech. Just think about some of the slang expressions that have swept this country after being heard a few times on radio or TV. In Britain the same thing has been happening with

6

other usages as well, though less consciously. People hear a certain pronunciation or expression over and over, and gradually they begin using it in place of the one they have been using.

Of course the smoothing out of British regional differences is not going to happen overnight. It will take many years. And until then, people in Britain will continue to do what they do now: They use their regional dialect with people of their own region, especially their families and friends. But when they communicate with people from other areas or when they know that using regionalisms might take a listener's attention away from what they are saying (because he is so interested in how they are saying it), they avoid regionalisms. They use instead words and expressions that are common to almost all areas of Britain.

We Americans also have regional dialects. Anyone who has heard the members of a professional football team being interviewed on radio or TV knows that the speech of the halfback from Pennsylvania does not sound exactly like the speech of the guard from Mississippi. And the speech of the Mississippi guard sounds different from the speech of both the center from Boston and the tackle from Iowa.

The differences in American speech are rooted in our history. The people who settled earliest along the Atlantic seaboard came mainly from various parts of England and spoke various regional dialects. In time the different dialects within a settled area blended and became what amounted to a new dialect. Because travel was difficult and because people were busy establishing a foothold in their new country, there was little communication between settled areas, especially between those that were any distance apart. So it is easy to see why the speakers of each area ended up with a different British blend — or, to put it another way, a slightly different American dialect.

Beginning in the early 1700's, groups of people began moving westward from the coastal settlements, taking with them the dialect of the area they came from. As time went on, more and more people pushed westward. Most of those from western New England and upper New York State moved into

7

the Great Lakes region and on into the Dakotas. People from the Middle Atlantic States headed west along the Ohio River and southwest through what is now West Virginia and Kentucky. Southerners went into Mississippi and parts of Texas. The last areas to be settled were the Rocky Mountain region and the West Coast, except of course for the part of California already settled by the Spanish. Lured by the good land to be had or the promise of finding silver or gold, people from all Eastern dialect regions headed for the Far West by land and by sea. Today traces of all American dialects are found there.

In the 1800's great numbers of non-English-speaking people began arriving in America. Some mixed with already settled groups. Others settled in separate communities, and though they quickly learned English, it was an English flavored by their native language. As industry grew, some of the new immigrant groups settled around steel mills, oil refineries, canning factories, and so on.

Every group that came to the United States contributed something to our language. The French who settled in Louisiana and the Spanish who settled in California and parts of the Southwest made substantial contributions. And of course the very first Americans contributed a good deal to our vocabulary. Many Indian names for things, especially unfamiliar plants, animals, and geographical features, were adopted.

Linguistic geographers—linguists who study regional dialectal differences—believe that today there are three major dialect regions: the Northern, the Midland, and the Southern. These parallel to some extent the paths of the Western migration. Within each of these regions, of course, there are minor dialect areas, as in New York City, New Orleans, and the Ozarks.

Some differences in regional pronunciation are quite noticeable; others are so subtle that only an expert can recognize them. But a Westerner traveling in Eastern New England, a distinct dialect area of the Northern region, would surely notice that speakers in this area pronounce the *a* in words like *ask*, *half*, and *path* with an "ah" sound. They also put an *r* between

8

vowel sounds. For example, when they say "the idea of" and "the law of," it sounds something like "the idear of" and "the lore of." On the other hand, they "drop" the /r/ sound in words like *eastern* ("eastuhn") and *appear* ("appeah").

In the Inland region, the western part of the Northern region, every *r* is firmly pronounced. A Southerner traveling in the upper Midwest quickly becomes aware not only of the strong /r/ sound but also of the "ah" sound in words like *on* and *block* and the /s/ sound in the words *grease* and *greasy* (where he uses a /z/ sound).

Like the Eastern New Englander, the Southern speaker tends to drop *r*'s. He also gives an "ah" sound to the long *i* in words like *I, my,* and *high.* And *Miss* and *Mrs.* he often pronounces /miz/.

Midland speech contains characteristics of both Northern and Southern regional speech. In fact, some linguistic geographers use the terms *Southern* Midland and *Northern* Midland in describing the speech of this region. But Midland also has some distinctive features of its own, like the intrusive *r* in the words *wash* ("worsh") and *Washington* ("Worshington").

A person who moves from one dialect region to another (or sometimes even within a major dialect region) soon learns that some of the names he uses for ordinary, everyday things are not the names commonly used there. What is a *faucet* in one area, for example, is a *spicket,* a *spigot,* or a *tap* in other areas. A certain kind of melon is called variously a *muskmelon,* a *mushmelon,* a *mussmelon,* a *cantaloupe,* a *lope.* Which of the following are used in your area?

> pancakes, batter cakes, hot cakes, griddlecakes, flannel cakes, flapjacks, slapjacks, fritters, flitters

> frying pan, skillet, spider, fry pan, creeper

> paper bag, sack, poke, tote bag

> lounge, couch, sofa, chesterfield, davenport

sitting room, parlor, front room, living room, bestroom, hall, keeping room

praying mantis, walking stick, darning needle, devil's horse

skip school, play hookey, bolt, hook Jack, play truant, bag school, ditch, flick, flake school

touchy, testy, feisty, fretful, touchous

quarter of ten, quarter to ten, quarter till ten, quarter before ten

Many of these regional words and expressions are gradually disappearing. There are several reasons why. In this century great numbers of people have moved from rural areas to large cities or metropolitan areas. Once there, to avoid having fun poked at their rural speech, they exchange words and expressions common in the small area they came from for the ones used in the new area. Newspapers, magazines, and national advertising have had a great influence. Readers who see the term *cottage cheese*, and only *cottage cheese*, used in articles on cooking and dieting and in advertisements gradually begin using that term in place of their *clabber cheese*, *curd cheese*, *Dutch cheese*, *sour-milk cheese*, *pot cheese*, or *smearcase*. And once they stop using the old regional name, it dies. Succeeding generations never hear it or know it.

Radio and TV have brought about changes in pronunciation as well as in vocabulary. Most announcers and commentators on the big networks sound alike. Consequently, Americans, who spend a good deal of time with radio and TV, tend little by little, consciously or unconsciously, to adopt what some people call "network English." And as in Britain, education has also played a part in smoothing out dialectal differences.

In a few places, however, the local dialect is still strong. One is an area in Pennsylvania settled by Rhineland Germans.

People there speak a dialect called Pennsylvania German or Pennsylvania Dutch, which has many distinctive idioms, like *got awake* for "awoke" or "woke up," *It wonders me* (meaning "It amazes me"), and *all* with the meaning "all gone; ended" ("The milk is all").

Another "dialect island" is in an area along the coast of South Carolina and Georgia, including the Sea Islands. There descendants of people brought from Africa in the early 1600's live and farm. The dialect that these people speak — Gullah — reflects strong influences of African languages. Most Americans have never heard Gullah spoken.

One thing should be kept in mind about the differences in American regional dialects, however. Though they exist, they are neither numerous nor great — and never were. American people who speak different regional dialects have no trouble communicating with each other. In fact, their speech has far more in common than not.

Besides their regional dialects, people also use other small, "specialized" dialects at certain times. Shoptalk, for example, is a kind of dialect, since it can serve to set one group of people apart from others. Truck drivers, computer programmers, engineers, printers, actors, skiers, ham-radio operators, gourmets all have their own shoptalk — "in-group" words and expressions that are not familiar to people outside the group. A similar kind of dialect is the slang that young people use in talking with each other.

In addition to regional and specialized dialects, everyone speaks a dialect of another kind. Linguists who study these dialects put them into two main categories — standard English and nonstandard English. Standard English they further divide into formal English and informal English. In general, standard English is the English used by educated people. Nonstandard English is the English used by people who have not had much education or who were not much affected by the schooling they did have.

These kinds of English are sometimes called "class dialects" or "social dialects." The term "class dialect" stems from the fact that people have made use of dialects in the same way people have made use of wealth or birth or special abilities — as a reason for feeling superior to others. For a prime example of this, let's go back to Britain.

Among the regional dialects that developed in Britain was the London dialect. By Shakespeare's time London had become the most prestigious city in Britain. It was the home of the government — the Court and Parliament. It was the largest seaport in the country and the center of commerce. Anyone who was anyone came to London. As the city's prestige grew, so did the prestige of its dialect. In the end, the London dialect became accepted as *the standard* dialect of Britain.

Of course no language stays the same. As time went on, the prestigious London dialect changed some. Many of the changes served to separate the way the "upper class" (nobility, wealthy people of very old families, high government officials, and so on) spoke from the way the "lower class" (shopkeepers, soldiers, sailors, servants, and so on) spoke. Hence, the term "class dialects."

Later a "middle class," comprised at first mainly of wealthy merchants and factory owners, came into being. And it wasn't long before members of the middle class, whose family origins were lower class, were ambitiously seeking a place in the upper class. As part of their campaign, they usually tried to make themselves sound "upper class" by acquiring the standard — the prestige — dialect.

In America, which never had the kind of class society that Britain had, the term "class dialect" can be misleading. "Social dialect," though rather vague, is somewhat better, since people do tend to associate more with people who speak the same dialect they do — standard or nonstandard. But whatever label is used, everyone would probably agree, whether they approve or not, that the prestige dialect in America is what linguists call the standard dialect.

As we noted earlier, linguists divide standard English into two kinds — formal English and informal English. Formal English is just what its name suggests; it is the kind of English educated people use on formal occasions — in an address to the UN, for example, or at a ceremony dedicating a new center for the performing arts. But formal English is used more often in writing than in speech, so you are more likely to read it than hear it. It is used in academic and technical writing (scholarly articles, reports on experiments, theses, legal documents) as well as in certain kinds of literature (certain kinds of essays, fiction, biography).

More familiar to most people is informal English. It is the kind of English educated people generally use for conversation and discussion. You hear it at a backyard barbecue, in the classroom, at a business conference, in a radio or TV interview with an athlete or a diplomat. Written informal English is the speech of educated people used with care. It is the English of most personal and business letters, newspaper and magazine articles, short stories, novels, and plays. If you speak standard English, informal English is your English.

Who determines what is standard usage? For example, look at the following pairs of sentences. Who determines that, because of the italicized usages they contain, one sentence gets labeled nonstandard and the other standard?

NONSTANDARD: Their dog *run* away.
STANDARD: Their dog *ran* away.

NONSTANDARD: *Him* and *me* are old friends.
STANDARD: *He* and *I* are old friends.

NONSTANDARD: She could*n't scarcely* talk.
STANDARD: She could *scarcely* talk.

Despite what some people think, standard usage is not dictated by a small group of dictionary makers or authors of textbooks on usage. On the contrary, standard usage is set by thousands of people — people skillful in using the language. Who are they? They are people who make our laws, run our government, handle our diplomatic relations, preside over our law courts. They are professionals—doctors, nurses, lawyers, teachers, actors. They write our books and our advertising. They publish our newspapers and magazines. They run our businesses and industries. They may be stockbrokers, sales-clerks, policemen, firemen, housewives, students, mechanics, farmers, printers, cooks.

People who think that standard usage is dictated from on high sometimes also have the idea that standard English is "good" and nonstandard English is "bad." It is true that standard English is the prestige dialect. But as far as language experts are concerned, a dialect is not in itself good *or* bad. In evaluating any kind of language, a linguist is concerned first of all with how well it conveys a speaker's intended meaning. In most everyday situations nonstandard English can convey meaning just as clearly as standard English. For evidence, look back at the labeled example sentences. Although some word forms differ, the meaning conveyed by the sentences in each pair is exactly the same. A linguist's second criterion is whether or not the language a speaker uses is appropriate to the situation in which he is using it. Let's consider what "appropriate to the situation" means.

All of us, without thinking about it, make changes in our language as we move from situation to situation. We adjust our language to fit the occasion. The language you use in talking with members of your family is unlikely to be exactly the same sort you would use in testifying in a law court. The way you greet an elderly neighbor you are not well acquainted with is likely to differ from the way you greet a close friend of your own age.

If you did not make adjustments like these, what would happen? Well, suppose that in testifying before a jury, you used very casual language and slang terms familiar only to your family and close friends. The jury might well get the impression that you did not take your testimony seriously and that you did not much care whether they understood or believed it. By making adjustments in the language we use—by making our language appropriate to the occasion—we avoid making impressions we don't want to make. We avoid letting how we are saying something distract attention from what we are saying.

The reason that users of nonstandard English are often urged to learn standard English is not that nonstandard is "bad" or that it does not communicate. The reason is that there are situations in which nonstandard is less appropriate than standard, where nonstandard may, in fact, make an impression a speaker does not intend or want.

Sometimes, especially if a user of nonstandard English has never been in such a situation, he assumes he never will be. He thinks he will never face any situations other than the ordinary everyday ones in which his nonstandard dialect serves him well enough. So he is not interested in learning standard English. And, of course, he is free not to.

But this person may be overlooking a few things. One is that the number of occupations that require frequent and skillful use of language—standard language—is increasing; occupations in which the use of language is not a factor are decreasing. Second, if he is like most people, he wants to be heard. He wants to express his views on politics, on foreign relations, on the environment, on the cost of living, on labor negotiations, on community matters. He might even someday want to run for public office. If so, he is likely to find nonstandard English inadequate for his needs. He is likely to find that he can reach more people and make his voice heard more effectively with standard English.

Actually there is no need to choose between standard and nonstandard English. A speaker can do what speakers of regional British dialects have been doing—use more than one dialect. When he is with people who use nonstandard English exclusively and who may feel uncomfortable with standard, he can use nonstandard if it comes naturally. But he will find it an advantage to learn standard English as well. It will come in handy in situations where it is the more appropriate dialect, where nonstandard usages might stand out.

If you have nonstandard usages in your speech and you want to be able to substitute standard usages for them, this book can help you. It is about the most common differences between the standard and nonstandard dialects. And you may discover that the differences are not as numerous as you thought. As with regional dialects, the similarities between social dialects far outnumber the differences.

This book consists of six "file drawers." In the first four you will find explanations of differences in standard and nonstandard use of verbs, subjects and verbs, pronouns, and modifiers. The fifth drawer contains discussions on the use and misuse of certain words and expressions — "dictional demons" that often trip people up. The items in the sixth drawer have to do with the "mechanics" of speaking and writing — capitalization, pronunciation, punctuation, spelling, and so on. The items explained in each section are arranged alphabetically.

Becoming aware of what the standard usage is, however, is just the first step. The next step is drill. For example, suppose you want to be able to substitute the standard *you were* for the nonstandard *you was*. Only by saying *you were* over and over in different sentences until it no longer sounds strange or different on your tongue will you be able to use it naturally. For this reason, you will find at the end of each section a generous supply of drill exercises. They will give you a start at acquiring the standard dialect.

FILE DRAWER 1

verb usage

ain't

Speakers of nonstandard English use *ain't* as a contraction for *am not, is not, are not, has not*, and *have not*.

Some authorities feel that *ain't* would be a useful addition to informal English as a contraction for *am not* in questions ("I'm supposed to sit here, ain't I?"), particularly since there is no established contraction for *am I not*. They point out that *amn't I* has never been generally accepted; and *aren't I*, which is accepted, is certainly no more grammatically "correct" than *ain't I*.

Nevertheless *ain't* remains nonstandard in all uses. And the furor that rose some years ago when the third edition of *Webster's New International Dictionary* noted that "many cultivated speakers" use *ain't I* for *am I not* would suggest that acceptance of *ain't* is unlikely or at least a long way off.

allow

In some local dialects the word *allow* is used to mean "think" or "say":

LOCALISM: He allowed it was too cold for the picnic.
STANDARD: He thought it was too cold for the picnic.

LOCALISM: I allowed that I agreed.
STANDARD: I said that I agreed.

borrow, lend

In standard English the verbs *borrow* and *lend* are used to mean two different things:

STANDARD: David borrowed a sweater from John.
[David got a sweater from John.]

STANDARD: John lent David a sweater.   [John gave David a sweater.]

A borrower "gets." A lender "gives."

In some regional dialects, however, *borrow* is used to mean "lend":

DIALECT: Will you borrow me a dollar?
STANDARD: Will you lend (*or* loan) me a dollar?

DIALECT: I borrowed him fifty cents.
STANDARD: I lent him fifty cents.

bring, take

The choice between *bring* and *take* depends on the direction of the action. When the motion is **toward** the speaker, a form of *bring* is used:

Bring me my boots and my saddle.

He often *brought* his little brother along when he came over.

When he called last night, Dad said he *was bringing* us some unusual souvenirs.

When the motion is **away from** the speaker, a form of *take* is used:

Take me out to the ball game.

He *should have taken* his little brother with him when he went home.

She *is taking* the coat back to the shop tomorrow.

bust

Speakers of nonstandard English often use *bust* where speakers of standard English use the verb *break* or *burst*:

> NONSTANDARD: How did Norman bust his arm?
> STANDARD: How did Norman break his arm?

> NONSTANDARD: The lock on the back door is busted.
> STANDARD: The lock on the back door is broken.

> NONSTANDARD: All of a sudden Shaughnessy busted out laughing.
> STANDARD: All of a sudden Shaughnessy burst out laughing.

The expressions *bust a bronco, bust a trust, bust an officer* (reduce in rank) are labeled *Slang* in some dictionaries. But they are so generally used in informal English that they may be considered standard.

graduate from

The formal and somewhat archaic idiom *to be graduated from* has generally been replaced by the shorter *graduate from*:

> RARE: My brother will be graduated from high school in June.
> USUAL: My brother will graduate from high school in June.

Some speakers of nonstandard English, perhaps influenced by advertisers who urge customers to "shop National" and "fly United," go a step further and drop the *from* (My brother will graduate high school in June). But speakers of standard English tend to avoid this usage.

had of

Speakers of nonstandard English often insert an unnecessary *of* after *had* (or its contraction *'d*) in clauses beginning with *if*:

> NONSTANDARD: If he had of taken my advice, he'd be president now.   [Or: If he'd of taken my advice.]
> STANDARD: If he had taken my advice, he'd be president now.   [Or: If he'd taken my advice.]

had ought

Had ought and *hadn't ought* are nonstandard forms of the standard *ought* and *ought not*:

> NONSTANDARD: She had ought to hire a lawyer.
> STANDARD: She ought to hire a lawyer.

> NONSTANDARD: They hadn't ought to spend so much money.
> STANDARD: They ought not (*or* oughtn't) to spend so much money.

Notice the *to* after *ought*; it should not be omitted:

> He oughtn't to act so cocky.   [Not: He oughtn't act.]

A good way to avoid problems with *ought* is to use *should* instead: He shouldn't act so cocky.

lay, lie

The following sentences are alike in two ways. First, each sentence contains a form of the verb *lay*, which means "put or place." Second, each sentence tells *what* or *who* is (or was) put or placed:

I usually *lay* the **keys** on the mantel.

The nurse *laid* the **baby** in the crib.

Someone *had laid* a sticky **lollipop** on the car seat.

Peg *was laying* **strips** of bacon in the big skillet.

Whenever the sentence tells what or who is placed somewhere, *lay* is the verb to use. These are its basic forms:

lay   laid   (has) laid   laying

Now look at these sentences. Each contains a form of the verb *lie*, which means "stretch out; recline; be in a flat position":

I always *lie* on the floor to watch TV.

He *lay* there all afternoon and slept.

Aldo *must have lain* in some poison ivy.

The cat *was lying* on the window ledge.

Whenever the sentence tells that someone or something is (or was) reclining or in a horizontal position, then *lie* is the verb to use. These are its basic forms:

lie   lay   (has) lain   lying

Users of nonstandard English tend to let *lay* (*laid, laid, laying*) do the work of both these verbs. The use of *laid* (the past tense of *lay*) instead of *lay* (the past tense of *lie*) is especially common: "He laid in the hammock all day." Even in everyday informal speech you will hear *lay* used instead of *lie* in a sentence like "Lay down, Rover." But in careful speech and writing, in both formal and informal English, the distinctions between *lay* and *lie* are observed.

learn, teach

Learn means "gain knowledge or skill." *Teach* means "show how to do; make understand; give instructions to." Nonstandard English often uses *learn* instead of *teach*:

> NONSTANDARD: Minnesota Fats learned him how to play pool.
> STANDARD: Minnesota Fats taught him how to play pool.
> STANDARD: He learned how to play pool from Minnesota Fats.

In standard English, both formal and informal, someone *teaches* you something, and you *learn* from him.

let, leave

The first line of a once-popular song goes: "*Let* me call you sweetheart; I'm in love with you." Notice the first word of the song. It is *Let* — not *Leave*. The meaning is "*Allow* me to call you sweetheart." If you, like the songwriter, get into the habit of using *let* whenever you mean "allow" or "permit," you will have no trouble with the troublesome *let-leave* verb pair.

Learn the first line of the song. *Let* it remind you that *let* is the right form to use in sentences like these:

> *Let* us help you.   [Not: *Leave* us help.]

> I *let* him drive for a while.   [Not: I *left* him drive.]

She *should have let* us help.   [Not: *should have left* us help.]

The other driver *had been letting* us ride free.   [Not: *had been leaving* us ride free.]

When the meaning is not "allow," *leave* is the verb to use:

I generally *leave* the house at seven.

He *had left* his suitcase at the airport.

With the word *alone,* either verb is standard idiomatic usage: "Leave him alone" or "Let him alone."

raise, rise

Raise (raised, raised, raising) takes an object:

My aunt in Miami *raises* **orchids** in her backyard.

He *raised* the **blind** and looked out.

Rise (rose, risen, rising) does not take an object:

No one can prove that the sun *will rise* tomorrow.

The cost-of-living index *rose* by half a point.

reckon

In some local dialects *reckon* is used to mean "think" or "suppose":

LOCALISM: Where do you reckon he went?
STANDARD: Where do you suppose he went?

remember

In standard English the preposition *of* is not used after the verb *remember*:

> NONSTANDARD: He said he didn't remember of borrowing the money.
> STANDARD: He said he didn't remember borrowing the money.

sit, set

The basic forms of the verb *sit* are —

> sit   sat   (has) sat   sitting

And the basic forms of *set* are —

> set   set   (has) set   setting

To decide whether the verb *sit* or *set* belongs in a particular sentence, use this simple procedure:

—If the sentence tells about someone sitting down, or sitting up, or sitting still, or sitting in the driver's seat, or sitting on pins and needles, use a form of *sit*:

> You *sit* by the window.

> Jack *can sit* on the aisle.

> Henry *sat* on his hands to keep them warm.

> I suppose I *should have sat* by Ruth.

> The bucket and mop *are* still *sitting* on the top step, right in everyone's way.

—If the sentence tells about someone putting something somewhere, use a form of *set*:

> *Set* the plant there.

> Who *set* the hot iron on the kitchen table?

> Ellen *had set* a pan on the floor under the leaking pipe.

> He *was setting* flowerpots over the plants to protect them from the rabbits.

In each of the "set" sentences, as you can see, there is a direct object—a word that tells what got set somewhere (the plant, the hot iron, a pan, flowerpots). But in the "sit" sentences, there are no direct objects.

suspicion

In standard English the word *suspicion* is used only as a noun (I had a suspicion that Henry wasn't telling the whole story). Its use as a verb is nonstandard. The standard verb is *suspect*.

> NONSTANDARD: I suspicioned him right away.
> STANDARD: I suspected him right away.

VERB FORMS: STANDARD AND NONSTANDARD

We use verbs not only to tell *what* action is done, but also to give an idea of *when* the action is done—

> Right now: I *work* for Mr. Peebles.

> The monkey *works* for peanuts.

> He *is working* his way through college.

In the past: Max *worked* at a filling station then.

But we *did work* hard!

The boys *were working* on their cars.

Al *has worked* at the glue factory for years.

They *should have been working* alone.

Several of the typists *had worked* overtime.

In the future: Elaine *will work* with me.

We *will be working* together.

On Friday Arthur *will have worked* here a month.

All twelve of these forms of the verb *work* are different. Yet all of them are made from four basic forms of the verb, called the *principal parts* of the verb:

1) the simple form, or infinitive: *work*

2) the past form: *worked* (used alone to show past time)

3) the past participle: *worked* (used with helping verbs like *has, have, had*)

4) the present participle: *working* (used with helping verbs like *is, were, have been*)

Notice that both the second and third principal parts of the verb *work* are made by adding *-ed* to the simple form. Verbs whose principal parts are built on this pattern are called *regular* verbs. Most English verbs are regular, like these:

SIMPLE FORM	PAST FORM	PAST PARTICIPLE
jump	jumped	(has) jumped
stay	stayed	(has) stayed

Unfortunately not all English verbs are regular. If they were, the number of problems people have with verb forms would be greatly reduced, since about 90 percent of verb-usage problems are caused by *irregular* verbs — verbs whose past form and past participle are not formed by adding *-ed*.

Take the irregular verbs *see*, *run*, and *do*, for example — three prime troublemakers:

SIMPLE FORM	PAST FORM	PAST PARTICIPLE
see	saw	(has) seen
run	ran	(has) run
do	did	(has) done

Two things often go wrong when people use these trouble-making verbs:

1) They use the past-participle forms *without a helping verb* (instead of using the past forms):

NONSTANDARD	STANDARD
I *seen* it myself.	I *saw* it myself.
Albert *run* for help.	Albert *ran* for help.
We *done* all the work.	We *did* all the work.

2) They use the past forms *with a helping verb* (instead of using the past-participle forms):

NONSTANDARD	STANDARD
You *should have saw* him.	You *should have seen* him.
My dog *has ran* away again.	My dog *has run* away again.
We *could have did* better.	We *could have done* better.

If you ever have trouble with verb forms, it is probably with one or more of the verbs in the following list of the most troublesome irregular verbs:

SIMPLE FORM	PAST FORM	PAST PARTICIPLE
be	was	(has) been
become	became	(has) become
begin	began	(has) begun
blow	blew	(has) blown
break	broke	(has) broken
bring	brought	(has) brought
choose	chose	(has) chosen
come	came	(has) come
do	did	(has) done
draw	drew	(has) drawn
drink	drank	(has) drunk
drive	drove	(has) driven
eat	ate	(has) eaten
fall	fell	(has) fallen
fly	flew	(has) flown
freeze	froze	(has) frozen
give	gave	(has) given
go	went	(has) gone
grow	grew	(has) grown
know	knew	(has) known
mistake	mistook	(has) mistaken
ride	rode	(has) ridden
ring	rang	(has) rung
rise	rose	(has) risen
shake	shook	(has) shaken
shrink	shrank, shrunk	(has) shrunk
sing	sang, sung	(has) sung
sink	sank, sunk	(has) sunk
speak	spoke	(has) spoken
spring	sprang, sprung	(has) sprung
steal	stole	(has) stolen

swear	swore	(has) sworn
swim	swam	(has) swum
take	took	(has) taken
tear	tore	(has) torn
throw	threw	(has) thrown
wear	wore	(has) worn
write	wrote	(has) written

VERB PROBLEMS WITH TIME

Two errors involving verb forms and time frequently crop up in nonstandard English:

1 Users of nonstandard English (and some users of standard English in the excitement of the moment) often begin telling a story in the past time and then somewhere in the middle suddenly shift to present, like this:

> ". . . Mr. Piper *was* still *waiting* at the bus stop when suddenly a cab *races* across the intersection. Just as he *notices* that nobody *seemed* to be at the wheel, he *hears* a scream."

Most people, having heard this much of the story, would wonder what had happened next. And many of them (users of standard English especially) would also wonder why the speaker was "spoiling" his story by using the verb forms he did. Every action he was telling about had happened *in the past.* Then why didn't he stick to past forms of the verbs instead of shifting from past to present? His story would have been just as interesting and would have sounded better and been easier to follow if he had been consistent:

> ". . . Mr. Piper *was* still *waiting* at the bus stop when suddenly a cab *raced* across the intersection. Just as he *noticed* that nobody *seemed* to be at the wheel, he *heard* a scream."

Sometimes, of course, there is a good reason for shifting from past to present in a single sentence. For example:

> Scientists *learned* many years ago that air *is* a mixture of gases.

Since the last part of the sentence states a fact that is always true, regardless of time, it is appropriate to use the present form *is*, even though the first verb is in the past. But remember that unless there is a good reason for shifting, you should keep the time of your verbs consistent.

2 In standard English the helping verb *had*—not *would have* or *would of*—is used in *if*-clauses and wishes referring to the past:

> NONSTANDARD: If you *would have asked* him, he would have lent you his.
> STANDARD: If you *had asked* him, he would have lent you his.

> NONSTANDARD: I wish I *would have been* there last night.
> STANDARD: I wish I *had been* there last night.

(See also **had of.**)

FILE I: PRACTICE 1.   *Be ready to read each of the following sentences aloud, using the verb in parentheses that would be used in standard English.*

1. Do you let the dog (*lay, lie*) on your bed?
2. Don't (*lay, lie*) in the sun too long.

3. You have (*laid, lain*) there for an hour already.
4. It rained, so we just (*laid, lay*) around watching TV.
5. He took off his coat and (*laid, lay*) it on the radiator to dry.
6. Rusty (*laid, lay*) down on the floor and went to sleep.
7. We had (*laid, lain*) money aside for just such an emergency.
8. He examined the photograph and (*laid, lay*) it carefully on the desk.
9. She pushed the branch aside, and there (*laid, lay*) Jimmy, fast asleep.
10. Please don't (*lay, lie*) in the hammock until we get it fixed.
11. Yesterday she just (*laid, lay*) around the house doing nothing.
12. Is that your bike (*laying, lying*) out there in the rain?
13. As soon as they left, Helen (*laid, lay*) the baby back in the crib.
14. The longer I (*laid, lay*) there, the less I felt like getting up.
15. As soon as they left, Mom (*laid, lay*) down again.
16. She shouldn't have (*laid, lain*) so close to the fire.
17. She shouldn't have (*laid, lain*) the doll so close to the fire.
18. (*Lay, Lie*) down awhile and rest.
19. He (*laid, lay*) there for an hour, trying to remember the details.
20. Are you going to (*lay, lie*) in bed all day?

FILE I: PRACTICE 2. *Be ready to read each of the following sentences aloud, substituting for the blank the appropriate form of* lay *or* lie.

1. Please don't _____ there, Tom; you're in the way.
2. He has been _____ on that cot while we've been working.
3. The money Grandpa had _____ aside had been stolen too.
4. I wish you wouldn't _____ on the floor.
5. _____ the rug down over there, Dave.
6. Do you realize how long you've been _____ there?

7. Half of the men in the steel mill have been _____ off.
8. Ron must have _____ awake all night.
9. There _____ his glasses, right where he had _____ them.
10. Somebody had been _____ in the hammock.
11. She had just _____ down to rest when Aunt Liz came over.
12. As soon as Aunt Liz left, Mom _____ down again.
13. He _____ on the beach all morning and caught a cold.
14. You're _____ on Dad's new jacket!
15. Is that your money _____ on the window sill?
16. How can I get past when you're _____ there in everybody's way?
17. Al shuts off the alarm and then _____ down again.
18. He was sure he had _____ his briefcase on the desk.
19. Bonnie had _____ in the sun two hours and was a bright lobster pink.
20. One of the motorcycles was _____ on its side in the mud.

FILE I: PRACTICE 3.   *Be ready to read each of the following sentences aloud, using the verb in parentheses that would be used in standard English.*

1. Yes, but his dad won't (*leave, let*) him drive the new car.
2. She had been (*leaving, letting*) us in for the children's admission.
3. I'd (*leave, let*) Eddie open his presents now.
4. (*Leave, Let*) me see them.
5. She shouldn't have (*left, let*) the baby by himself so long.
6. Miss Connors always (*leaves, lets*) us pick our own topics.
7. He wouldn't even (*leave, let*) me explain.
8. Mom won't (*leave, let*) us eat between meals.
9. If you hear anything more, (*leave, let*) me know.
10. (*Leave, Let*) go of that handle!
11. Let's (*leave, let*) the rest go until tomorrow.

12. Why don't you (*leave*, *let*) your little brother rake for a while?
13. You (*left*, *let*) that porch light burning again.
14. We (*left*, *let*) the car parked in their driveway.
15. We (*left*, *let*) him park their car in our driveway.
16. He (*left*, *let*) me standing there with my mouth open.
17. He (*left*, *let*) me stand there looking like a fool.
18. Let's (*leave*, *let*) Jerry paint the railing.
19. Why are you (*leaving*, *letting*) me do all the talking?
20. He doesn't even (*leave*, *let*) his wife use that new fishing rod of his.

FILE I: PRACTICE   4.   *Be ready to read each of the following sentences aloud, substituting for the blank the appropriate form of* let *or* leave.

1. Won't the store _____ you buy now and pay later?
2. No, her husband wouldn't _____ her keep the hat.
3. "_____ me in!" he shouted.
4. They won't _____ you in without a pass.
5. They aren't _____ anyone in who doesn't know the password.
6. Why are you _____ him boss you around again?
7. Dad won't _____ anybody sit in his lounge chair.
8. _____ Ben pay for himself for a change.
9. Aunt Min believes in _____ Eddie have his own way.
10. Don't wipe the glasses; just _____ them on the drainboard.
11. If I hear his side of the story, I'll _____ you know.
12. You can _____ your umbrella on the porch.
13. You can _____ your umbrella dry on the porch.
14. Hawkins _____ that grounder go right through his legs.
15. Why did he _____ the children play in the street?
16. _____ the window open, please.
17. Why don't you _____ your sister have the first choice?
18. I wouldn't _____ him talk back to me like that.

19. Donnie won't _____ anyone ride his bike.
20. Don't _____ Jennie see you crying.

FILE I: PRACTICE 5. *Be ready to read each of the following sentences aloud, using the verb form in parentheses that would be used in standard English.*

1. I wonder what (*become, became*) of that old razor of Dad's.
2. Pete has (*wrote, written*) the first draft, but it's terrible.
3. We (*begun, began*) to think they would never go home.
4. Just how much money was (*stole, stolen*)?
5. Have you (*spoke, spoken*) to them about the noise?
6. I had to borrow his pencil; mine was (*broke, broken*).
7. They (*done, did*) all they could to help.
8. Poor Dad has (*rode, ridden*) the bus all week.
9. The torte should be (*ate, eaten*) while it's fresh.
10. The paint around the handles had already (*wore, worn*) off.
11. Haven't you (*drank, drunk*) that milk yet?
12. By then my hands and feet were (*froze, frozen*).
13. A corner of the photograph had been (*tore, torn*) off.
14. Do you remember the movie we (*seen, saw*) in Denver?
15. Emil (*done, did*) most of the work.
16. If I had (*knew, known*) how, I would have (*drove, driven*) the bus myself.
17. Have you (*wrote, written*) your report for history yet?
18. The horse I had (*chose, chosen*) came in last.
19. I was sure he hadn't (*stole, stolen*) the money.
20. Linda hasn't (*spoke, spoken*) to Blair for a week.

FILE I: PRACTICE 6. *Be ready to read each of the following sentences aloud, using the verb form in parentheses that would be used in standard English.*

1. Five years later he (*became, become*) president of the firm.
2. Who had (*stole, stolen*) the pearls?

3. Bobby must have (*fell, fallen*) off his bicycle.
4. Then Bobby's mother (*began, begun*) to scream.
5. The handle had been (*broke, broken*) off.
6. Do you think my cheeks are (*froze, frozen*)?
7. My cousins had (*drove, driven*) over with the Rizzos.
8. The tardy bell hasn't (*rang, rung*) yet, has it?
9. I (*drank, drunk*) my milk, but Joe hasn't (*drank, drunk*) his.
10. When Ellen (*saw, seen*) the mouse, she screamed bloody murder.
11. You must have (*tore, torn*) your pants on that nail.
12. He has (*wore, worn*) that same shirt four days in a row.
13. I had (*wrote, written*) my address on the wrong line.
14. Yes, but has he ever (*drove, driven*) a semi?
15. Mr. Stein had (*gave, given*) Ron an old TV.
16. We had (*rode, ridden*) down there in an elegant limousine.
17. At that point Mr. Hull (*came, come*) in and ordered us out of the place.
18. Have you ever (*went, gone*) to an auction?
19. I know I wouldn't have (*chose, chosen*) that hideous tie.
20. Sharon wished she had (*wore, worn*) her blond wig.

FILE I: PRACTICE 7. *Each of the following sentences has one or two nonstandard verb forms. Be ready to read the sentences aloud, substituting standard forms for the nonstandard ones.*

1. It was the first raw oyster that Millie had ever ate.
2. I had never went to an opera before.
3. If he had wore a cap, his ears wouldn't have froze.
4. Luckily, no one seen us sneaking out.
5. The shirt was tore in two places.
6. Harold run over to see them yesterday.
7. Have you ever rode a pony?
8. The baby had fell down again.
9. You should have spoke to the manager.
10. The letter was wrote in green ink.
11. The vase I had broke turned out to be her favorite, of course.

12. What become of your cousin from Boston?
13. At any rate, I had did my best.
14. He done the best he could, too.
15. You shouldn't have gave him one cent.
16. Who rung that bell?
17. Mother must have took my sweater.
18. He had chose vanilla, and the waitress had brang chocolate.
19. I could have swore it was Frank.
20. She wondered if Lenny had stole the money.

FILE I: PRACTICE 8. *Be ready to read each of the following sentences aloud, using the verb in parentheses that would be used in standard English.*

1. Gene (*learned, taught*) me all I know about airplanes.
2. Don't let him (*set, sit*) in your dad's chair.
3. You (*had ought, ought*) to write her a thank-you note.
4. When did your brother (*graduate, graduate from*) Bradford High?
5. I don't (*remember of, remember*) turning off the gas.
6. The cat and the dog just (*set, sat*) there and stared at each other.
7. If she (*had of, had*) married Mr. Spence, she'd be a millionaire now.
8. He can't (*learn, teach*) you anything if you won't listen.
9. Clif would be here now if he (*would have, had*) flown.
10. Then I asked him to (*borrow, lend*) me a quarter.
11. None of us (*suspicioned, suspected*) Mrs. Dorsey.
12. When you go to Montreal, (*bring, take*) George a message from us.
13. My cousin is (*learning, teaching*) me trigonometry.
14. Don (*busted, broke*) the crystal when he dropped his watch.
15. The hem should be (*raised, risen*) an inch or so.
16. His father sat in the front row, just (*busting, bursting*) with pride.
17. I wish I (*had, would have*) won the portable TV instead.

18. Don't you think he (*had ought, ought*) to admit his mistakes?
19. Before I leave, I must (*bring, take*) this trash out to the garbage can.
20. Sally kept asking her dad to (*bring, take*) her to one of the hockey games.

FILE I: PRACTICE 9. *Each of the following sentences has a nonstandard verb form. Be ready to read the sentences aloud, substituting standard forms for the nonstandard ones.*

1. Spotty was laying there, right in the middle of the puddle.
2. Why did you leave him talk you into such a deal?
3. I finally asked the boss if he could borrow me a dollar until payday.
4. Terry suspicioned Mr. Flint from the beginning.
5. I wish Belinda would have seen me make that touchdown.
6. The two younger men had busted out of the prison camp before.
7. Please don't lay on the sofa with your shoes on.
8. Four or five cowboys were setting on the fence.
9. Don't you think he had ought to pay us a *little* reward at least?
10. Let's learn this smart aleck a lesson.
11. He's as ugly as sin, ain't he?
12. The second blast busted the windows of the supermarket.
13. Why don't you set in a more comfortable chair?
14. No, she won't leave anyone drive her car.
15. If I had of been there, I would have complained.
16. Miss Martin made me copy my paper in ink and then gives me a failing grade anyhow.
17. Didn't he graduate college last year?
18. Bud wouldn't leave me pay for my ticket.
19. By this time I realized that Hal didn't remember of borrowing that dollar from me.
20. Prices haven't raised at Eddie's Grill, have they?

FILE I: PRACTICE 10. A RE-DRILL. *Each of the following sentences has one or two nonstandard verb forms. Be ready to read the sentences aloud, substituting standard forms for the nonstandard ones.*

1. All of a sudden he seen us two setting there.
2. Uncle Lou must have came in through the basement window.
3. I wondered why Corey had went home without his guitar.
4. Frank said he run a mile when he seen the ghost.
5. If I would have been Mr. Pine, I would have rang the dismissal bell early.
6. She finally begun to calm down.
7. Normally he wouldn't have gave it a second look.
8. I wish I would have wore my storm coat.
9. "How tall you have grew," she said to Harold.
10. Have you ever drove in the mountains?
11. Mrs. Porter, who had never flew before, was quite nervous.
12. Just one hour of waiting on tables, and I was wore out.
13. My brother had swam over to the raft with the message.
14. You should have took a sweater along.
15. Lorraine said someone must have fell through the ice.
16. Tina had never drank papaya juice before.
17. Dad would have chose the sports model.
18. Mr. Sanders has drove that same old panel truck for years.
19. Why don't you leave him do it his way?
20. I hope they haven't froze; it was mighty cold last night.

FILE I: PRACTICE 11. A RE-DRILL. *Be ready to read each of the following sentences aloud, using the verb in parentheses that would be used in standard English.*

1. How much do you (*reckon, suppose*) that cost?
2. At first Mrs. Leal (*suspicioned, suspected*) her secretary.
3. Don't you (*remember, remember of*) getting an overdue notice?

4. Those experiments taught us that most metals (*expand, expanded*) with heat.
5. The figurine toppled over and (*broke, busted*) into a dozen pieces.
6. No, this (*ain't, isn't*) a legal holiday.
7. I just wish he (*would have, had*) called on George.
8. Finally Pete looked up and (*starts, started*) to laugh.
9. If you (*had of, had*) seen Bruno, you would have laughed too.
10. Just as he was reeling that huge pickerel in, the line (*breaks, broke*).
11. If Ben (*had of, had*) been there, he'd know these reports are accurate.
12. I'd (*allow, say*) the meeting won't start till eight.
13. I am the man you are looking for, (*ain't I, am I not*)?
14. Mrs. Farr's white gloves had been (*laid, lain*) right on the paint.
15. Don't you (*reckon, suppose*) he'll be back?
16. I soon realized that he (*suspicioned, suspected*) me.
17. Please (*bring, take*) these peaches to Mrs. Brodda, but (*bring, take*) back the basket.
18. Sam (*run, ran*) up to the door, (*rung, rang*) the bell, and then (*ducks, ducked*) out of sight.
19. You (*hadn't ought, ought not*) to criticize a book you haven't read.
20. She opened her purse, rummaged through it, and then (*hands, handed*) him a penny.

FILE I: PRACTICE 12. A RE-DRILL. *Each of the following sentences has two nonstandard verb forms. Be ready to read the sentences aloud, substituting standard forms for the nonstandard ones.*

1. The minute he seen me he begun to laugh.
2. Monty swum under water two full lengths before he come up for air.
3. Someone had broke in and had stole Pete's coin collection.

4. Al had ate a handful of cookies and had drank a quart of milk.
5. The idea come to him while he was laying on the beach.
6. Grandpa won't leave anyone set on the porch swing.
7. Why don't you leave Ross learn you how to do a swan dive?
8. I didn't suspicion that he was the one who had broke the window.
9. Jack laid the air mattress on the rocks, laid down on it, and begun practicing his speech.
10. He had just ran a block or two, and his heart begun to pound.
11. Ain't those your socks laying on the table?
12. Last week I borrowed him my skis and he busted them.
13. When Officer Brady come in the front door, Bill run out the back.
14. That handle is broke, ain't it?
15. I could have swore that she was the one who had spoke in assembly.
16. You had ought to tell him that the gate latch is broke.
17. I wish I would have went home before it begun to snow.
18. That will learn him not to leave his skates laying on the stairs.
19. She told us Dave had fell and had tore his jacket.
20. I quickly seen that he didn't remember of promising me a job.

FILE I: PRACTICE 13. A RE-DRILL. *Be ready to read each of the following sentences aloud, using the verb in parentheses that would be used in standard English.*

1. Hasn't Walter (*wrote, written*) that application letter yet?
2. If you hear anything else about it, (*leave, let*) me know.
3. As usual, the three of them were just (*setting, sitting*) around talking shop.
4. To tell the truth, Jane hasn't (*drove, driven*) since that accident last week.

5. Let's (*leave, let*) Uncle Jerry pay for the hamburgers and cokes this time.
6. The wind had (*tore, torn*) the shingles from the roof of the Petersons' house.
7. An hour later we (*began, begun*) to think he would never stop talking.
8. Yesterday Sharon just (*lay, laid*) around the house doing nothing at all.
9. In fact, I had the feeling that everyone there (*suspicioned, suspected*) me.
10. By twelve-thirty we (*began, begun*) to wish we (*had, would have*) taken the train.
11. "I think you (*had ought, ought*) to apologize to Mr. Kelso," she repeated.
12. If I (*had, would have*) known they were coming, I would have made a big pot of chili.
13. (*Bring, Take*) your workbooks when you leave, but (*bring, take*) them back to class tomorrow.
14. Corby (*graduated, graduated from*) St. Norbert's in June and went right to work at his father's store.
15. That's the second plate-glass window those fellows have (*busted, broken*) this week.
16. He's one teacher who (*learned, taught*) us to think for ourselves.
17. The lawn mower must have been (*stole, stolen*) while they were away on vacation.
18. Joe wouldn't have (*ran, run*) up those stairs if he (*had of, had*) realized the principal was watching.
19. Don't (*leave, let*) anyone (*lay, lie*) on the new sofa.
20. Phil must have (*went, gone*) to the corner to get a paper.

subject-verb agreement

FILE DRAWER 2

AGREEMENT OF SIMPLE SUBJECT AND VERB

The "rule" of subject-verb agreement is that a verb should agree with its subject in number. Or, to put it another way: In a standard English sentence a singular verb is used with a singular subject, and a plural verb is used with a plural subject. It sounds simple, doesn't it? Even so, from time to time almost everyone has trouble getting subjects and verbs matched up correctly. Why?

If during the next few days you listen to people talk — at home, at school, at work, on the street, on radio, on TV — and pay attention to the subjects and verbs in the sentences they use, you will get a good idea of why mistakes occur. You will discover, for instance, that when a subject and verb come close together in a sentence, mistakes are hardly ever made.

PEOPLE CORRECTLY SAY:

A *quart* **seems** more than enough for four servings. [Singular subject, singular verb.]

The *story* **has been told** many times.   [Singular subject, singular verb.]

But when the subject and verb are separated by a phrase or a clause, mistakes are common.

PEOPLE INCORRECTLY SAY:

A *quart* of strawberries **seem** more than enough for four servings.   [Singular subject, but plural verb. The verb should be singular — *seems.*]

The *story* of the great hardships men underwent on these expeditions **have been told** many times.   [Singular subject, but plural verb. The verb should be singular — *has been told.*]

What is it about these sentences that trips people up? In the first sentence it is the plural noun *strawberries*. In the second sentence it is the plural noun *expeditions*. A plural noun coming right before the verb often throws people off and causes them to use a plural verb, even though the subject is singular.

Special troublemakers are parenthetical phrases beginning with such prepositions as *together with, as well as, with, like, in addition to,* and *along with.* There is often a great temptation to use a plural verb in sentences like these:

> His *footprint*, together with the other clues, **proves** he is guilty.   [Not: *prove.*]

> The head *bookkeeper*, as well as the teller and the guard, **was fired.**   [Not: *were fired.*]

If a singular verb after such a phrase sounds "wrong" to you, it may be because the meaning seems obviously plural, as here:

> My father, together with my two uncles, **was working** hard to get the hay into the barn before the storm broke.

By changing the *together with* to *and* and then using a plural verb, you can emphasize the plural meaning and make a better-sounding sentence:

> My *father* AND my two *uncles* **were working** hard to get the hay into the barn before the storm broke.

Of course the problem isn't always with singular subjects and verbs. When a phrase ending with a singular noun comes between a plural subject and its verb, the subject and verb are also likely to be mismatched:

> INCORRECT: The *results* of the survey **shows** a majority of the employees in favor of the changes in work rules. [Plural subject, singular verb.]

CORRECT: The *results* of the survey **show** a majority of the employees in favor of the changes in work rules. [Plural subject, plural verb.]

Still another agreement problem comes up in sentences in which the simple subject and the predicate complement (which refers to the same person or thing as the subject) are of different number. But here, too, the usual agreement rule applies; the verb should agree with the subject, not with the predicate complement:

The *mosquitoes* **were** the greatest problem.   [Plural subject, plural verb.]

The greatest *problem* **was** the mosquitoes.   [Singular subject, singular verb.]

AGREEMENT: WITH "A NUMBER OF"; "THE NUMBER OF"

A plural verb is used with **a** *number*, meaning "several" or "many":

A number of accidents **have occurred** at that corner.

A singular verb is used with **the** *number*, meaning "the quantity" or "the total":

The number of accidents there **is** appalling.

AGREEMENT: WITH INDEFINITES

The words *each, every, either, neither, everyone, everybody, anyone, anybody, someone, somebody, no one, nobody* — called "indefinites" — are considered grammatically singular. Therefore when these words are used as subjects (or to modify subjects, simple or compound), singular verbs are used:

> I have checked both clocks, and neither **is** accurate.

> Every house and store on that block **belongs** to him.

> Then each delegate **signs** the document.

Do not let a plural noun following one of these words trick you into making the verb plural:

> Neither of the clocks **keeps** accurate time. [Not: *keep*.]

> Every one of those houses and stores **needs** some repair work. [Not: *need*.]

> Then each of the delegates **signs** the document. [Not: *sign*.]

> **Does** either of your brothers **play** guitar? [Not: *Do*.]

AGREEMENT: WITHIN RELATIVE CLAUSES

The verb in the relative clause following *one of those who* (or *which* or *that*) agrees in number with the antecedent of the pronoun *who*:

> Phyllis is one of those *people* who always **laugh** at their own jokes. [The antecedent of *who* is *people*. The meaning is "Of those people who always laugh at their own jokes, Phyllis is one."]

> Al is the only *one* of those boys who **has** ever **held** a job. [The antecedent of *who* is *one*. The meaning is "Of those boys, Al is the only one who has ever held a job."]

COLLECTIVE NOUNS

A *collective* noun is one that names a "collection" — or group — of persons or things:

audience	crew	herd
band	crowd	jury
chorus	faculty	majority
class	family	team
committee	flock	troup

A collective noun may take either a singular or a plural verb, depending on the meaning you want to convey. If you want to show that you are thinking of the group as a whole, as a single unit, use a singular verb:

The *band* **is** sure to win the state music competition.

The nominating *committee* **was meeting** at that very moment.

If you want to show that you are thinking of the individual members making up the group, use a plural verb:

The *band*, as usual, **were straggling** into the auditorium in groups of two or three.

The *committee* **were** still **arguing** about the wording of the report.

The use of a plural verb after a collective noun is more common in British English than in American English. In a British newspaper you might read, "The government *have* been considering the proposal for some weeks." In a U.S. newspaper, *has* would be used. Since the singular is more usual in the United States, a sentence like "The band were straggling into the auditorium" sounds "wrong" or "funny" to some people. So they avoid using *band* as a plural by inserting the word *members*: "The band members were straggling into the auditorium in groups of two or three"; "The members of the committee were still arguing about the wording of the report."

COMPOUND SUBJECTS WITH "AND"

A plural verb is generally used with a two-part subject joined by *and* or *both . . . and*:

> The owner and the editor **determine** the policy of the paper.   [Two people.]

> Both the costume and the wig **were rented** from Pop's Prop Shop.

But when the parts of a compound subject refer to the same person or thing, or are thought of as a unit, a singular form of the verb is used:

> The owner and editor, Ethel Mendez, **writes** the editorials.   [One person.]

> Macaroni and cheese **tastes** best when it's piping hot.   [Thought of as one item of food.]

> The stress and strain **was beginning** to undermine his health.

When a whole compound subject with *and* is modified by the indefinite *each* or *every*, a singular verb is used:

> Each name, address, and telephone number **has been verified**.

> Every man, woman, and child **was inoculated**.

COMPOUND SUBJECTS WITH "OR"

Although the subject of the following sentence has two parts, it is considered singular:

> In Mrs. Bard's absence, *Smith* or *Jensen* takes charge of the office.

In a sentence like this, it is the meaning, not the number of parts, that determines whether the subject is singular or plural. Here the word *or* shows that only *one* of the men takes charge — sometimes Smith, sometimes Jensen. When the parts of a compound subject joined by *or* or *nor* (or *either . . . or*, *neither . . . nor*) are singular, the subject is considered singular and takes a singular verb:

> *Patty, Maxine,* OR *Laverne* **is going** to help.

> NEITHER his *answer* NOR *mine* **was** right.

But in informal usage, especially in questions and in negative sentences, the verb is often plural when the subject is plural in idea:

> **Do** *Roger* OR *Dennis* always **win**?   [Formal: *Does.*]

> NEITHER the *doctor* NOR the *nurse* **were notified**.
> [Formal: *was notified.*]

When the parts of a compound subject joined by *or* or *nor* are plural or the part nearer the verb is plural, a plural verb is used:

> *Hamburgers* OR *wieners* **were** all she ever served.

> EITHER *George* OR the *twins* **have paid** the bill.
> But: EITHER the *twins* OR *George* **has paid** the bill.

Many writers think sentences like the last sound awkward, and phrase the idea in another way:

Either the twins have paid the bill, or George has.

In sentences like the following, the verb agrees with the affirmative part, not the negative:

You, not I, are invited.   I, not you, am invited.

Most writers would avoid the problem by rewording such sentences:

You are invited, not I.   I am invited, not you.

"HE DOESN'T" OR "HE DON'T"?

It is hardly likely that anyone you know ever makes a mistake in verb agreement in sentences like these:

Leo **does** most of the work.   [Singular subject, singular verb.]

The *boys* **do** most of the work.   [Plural subject, plural verb.]

Yet you very likely know a number of people who do make a mistake in verb agreement in sentences like the following:

THEY SAY: Leo **don't** like spinach.
The suit **don't** fit.
She **don't** live here any more.

THEY SHOULD SAY: Leo **doesn't** like spinach.
The suit **doesn't** fit.
She **doesn't** live here any more.

Why do people who never say "he do" (instead of "he does") say "he don't" (instead of "he doesn't")? The reason probably is that they have so often heard others say "he don't" that they have picked up the "he don't" habit themselves. And having heard — and said — "he don't" so often, it sounds right to them, even though it is nonstandard.

The best way to get rid of the "he don't" habit — if you have acquired it — is to substitute for it the "he doesn't" habit. As a starter, try reading aloud the following drill sentences. Then make it a point to repeat the sentences (or others like them) once or twice a day until "he doesn't" sounds right to you and "he don't" sounds wrong.

The TV doesn't work.	Doesn't that pie look good?
The iron doesn't work.	Doesn't the room feel chilly?
The stove doesn't work.	Doesn't she ever smile?
The motor doesn't work.	Doesn't Tom look happy?
The switch doesn't work.	Doesn't it look like rain?
He doesn't work.	Doesn't it make a difference?

SINGULAR OR PLURAL IN MEANING

A singular verb is used with words like *most, some, all, two thirds, half,* and *part* when they answer the question "How much?"

> *Most* of her report **was written** in red ink.   [*How much* of her report was written in red ink? *Most* of it.]

> *Two thirds* of the club **owes** dues.   [*How much* of the club owes dues? *Two thirds* of it.]

A plural verb is used when the words answer the question "How many?"

> *Most* of her reports **were written** in red ink.   [*How many* of her reports were written in red ink? *Most* of them.]

> *Two thirds* of the members **owe** dues.   [*How many* of the members owe dues? *Two thirds* of them.]

Often a phrase following a subject like *most* or *two thirds* gives an additional clue. If the phrase ends with a singular word like *report* or *club*, the subject usually tells "How much?" If the phrase ends with a plural like *reports* or *members*, the subject usually tells "How many?"

SUBJECTS: FORM vs. MEANING

1 Nouns like *codes*, *secrets*, and *spies* are plural both in form and in meaning; each names more than one. But nouns like *mumps*, *rickets*, *statistics*, *physics*, *checkers*, and *horseshoes* — which are also plural in form — actually have a singular meaning. Each is used as the name of a single thing: a disease, a science, a game. Since they are singular in meaning, they take singular verbs:

> *Mumps* **was** the only childhood disease I had.

> *Statistics* **is** a branch of mathematics.

> After chess, *checkers* **seems** monotonous.

2 When the subject of a sentence names a single unit of measure or time, it is usually considered singular — even though it is plural in form — and takes a singular verb:

> *Four and a half acres* certainly **does** not **provide** enough space.

Seven dollars **was** a reasonable price, he thought.

Thirty minutes **is** too long for that job.

3 Sometimes the subject of a sentence is the title of a book, article, poem, movie, program, painting, or song, or the name of a country, organization, or business firm. Though the title or name may contain plural words, a singular verb is used with it, since it is considered the name of one thing:

"American Names" **tells** why the poet likes the sound of many American names.

Kelly's Heroes **was** the late movie last night.

The Netherlands **is** the next country they will visit.

Charles Wingate's Sons **manufactures** ink.

VERB BEFORE SUBJECT

Ordinarily the subject of a sentence comes before the verb. But there are some kinds of sentences in which the verb (or part of the verb) comes before the subject. Getting the right verb — singular or plural — in sentences like these can be tricky.

1 Be on your guard when you begin a sentence with *Here* or *There*. The verb will probably come before the subject, so think ahead to the subject. If it is singular, make the verb singular:

There **is** another *box* of popsicles in the freezer.   [Or: *There's* another box.]

Here **is** your *third* of the profits.   [Or: *Here's* your third.]

There **was** a *wreath* OR a *candle* in every window.

59

But if the subject is going to be plural, make the verb plural:

There **are** a few *corrections* still to be made.   [Not: *is.*]

Here **are** the X-acto *knives* for the craft classes.   [Not: *is.*]

There **were** several *cartons* AND a *trunk* to be picked up.

Note: When the first part of a compound subject following *There* is singular, informal English often uses a singular verb:

There *was* a trunk and several cartons to be picked up.

In speech people frequently use the contractions *There's* and *Here's* before both singular and plural subjects, and it goes unnoticed. But in writing, where contractions are less often used and the number of the subject is more obvious, a singular verb with a plural subject will be noticed.

2 Questions, too, have to be watched, since the verb (or part of it) is likely to come before the subject. Be sure the verb you use matches the subject:

SINGULAR SUBJECTS, SINGULAR VERBS:

Does *either* of them **know** the address?   [Not: *Do.*]

Has your *brother* OR your *cousin* ever **been** to camp before?   [Not: *Have.*]

PLURAL SUBJECTS, PLURAL VERBS:

Where **are** the spare *parts*?   [Not: *Where is* or *Where's.*]

Were there enough *sandwiches*?   [Not: *Was.*]

Do *she* AND her *sister* still **work** at the hospital?   [Not: *Does.*]

3 "Inverted" sentences, those in which the subject is placed after the verb, can also be troublesome. A noun that is not the subject (even though it comes before the verb) may trick you into an error. Think ahead. Determine what the subject is going to be and make the verb either singular or plural to agree with it:

SINGULAR SUBJECTS, SINGULAR VERBS:

Among the prizewinning exhibits **was** a *collection* of drawings done by ghetto children.   [Not: *were*.]

After the cheerleaders and the pompon girls **comes** the *car* with the queen and her court.   [Not: *come*.]

PLURAL SUBJECTS, PLURAL VERBS:

At the bottom of the box **were** the flash *cubes* and the extra *lenses*.   [Not: *was*.]

Then around the corner **come** two more fire *trucks*. [Not: *comes*.]

"YOU WAS" OR "YOU WERE"?

In standard English the verb form *was* is used with singular subjects. The form *were* is used with plural subjects — and with the pronoun *you*, even if it refers to only one person.

NONSTANDARD: *You* **was** right, **was**n't *you*?
STANDARD: *You* **were** right, **were**n't *you*?

NONSTANDARD: The *presents* **was**n't for him; *they* **was** for me.
STANDARD: The *presents* **were**n't for him; *they* **were** for me.

Perhaps you have picked up the habit of saying "you was" (and "we was" and "they was") instead of "you were" (and "we were" and "they were"). If you sincerely want to get rid of the habit, you can. Spend a few minutes each day repeating sentences like the following ones. Keep up this daily drill for a week or so (longer if necessary). Soon you will find that "you were" and "we were" and "they were" sound "right" to you, and you will use them without thinking.

You were lucky, weren't you?

Where were the boys?

We were there.

We were early; they were late.

Where were you?

FILE II: PRACTICE 1. *Be ready to read each of the following sentences aloud, using the verb form in parentheses that agrees with the subject.*

1. This deck of cards (*has, have*) never been used.
2. The seats in the center section of the balcony (*is, are*) reserved for the parents.
3. The wax on both those floors (*has, have*) yellowed.
4. The scars on his left arm (*seems, seem*) to be fading finally.
5. Her interest in the band concerts these days (*surprises, surprise*) me.
6. Uncle Bob's favorite dessert (*is, are*) cream puffs.

7. The canoe, as well as the kitchen supplies, (*is*, *are*) to go by truck.
8. The directions on the back of the package (*tells*, *tell*) how much to use.
9. By this time the bus driver, as well as the passengers, (*was*, *were*) worried.
10. The profits on this one item alone (*amounts*, *amount*) to a tremendous sum.
11. The first row of seats (*was*, *were*) moved to make room for the orchestra.
12. Candy containing raisins or nuts (*gets*, *get*) stale quickly.
13. Mr. Scott, like all his employees, (*works*, *work*) until five.
14. The starch on the collar and cuffs (*makes*, *make*) red marks on my neck and wrists.
15. A set of mixing bowls (*is*, *are*) not my idea of an exciting gift.
16. A large carton of toys and books (*was*, *were*) shipped last Friday.
17. The greatest temptation for me (*was*, *were*) the homemade biscuits and bread.
18. Not one pair of all those socks (*was*, *were*) the right color.
19. Any novel about Hollywood celebrities (*interests*, *interest*) her.
20. A representative from each of the homerooms (*attends*, *attend*) these weekly meetings.

FILE II: PRACTICE 2.   *Be ready to read each of the following sentences aloud, using the verb form in parentheses that agrees with the subject.*

1. Yes, the committee (*has*, *have*) already turned in its report.
2. The speed with which those five men put up the walls (*was*, *were*) amazing.
3. The black eyes Paul got in his fight with Dave hardly (*improves*, *improve*) his looks.
4. The bowl of flowers (*is*, *are*) to be raffled off later.

5. One quart of strawberries (*was, were*) all they had.
6. The blouse with the red squiggles (*looks, look*) best with your skirt.
7. This column of numbers (*adds, add*) up to 500.
8. My cousin Mickey, like his father and brothers, (*has, have*) red hair and a terrible temper.
9. His serving of scrambled eggs and bacon (*was, were*) enough for three ordinary people.
10. The polka dots on his new tie (*clashes, clash*) with the stripes on his shirt.
11. A carton of baseballs (*was, were*) found in an open locker.
12. The main point made in both the speeches (*was, were*) the same.
13. The team (*was, were*) kidding each other about their long sideburns.
14. The spelling of all of the names on those cards (*has, have*) to be checked.
15. The camera, together with the carrying case, (*is, are*) yours for fifteen dollars.
16. That box of toys that Frank brought Jimmy and Ted (*has, have*) been sitting in the basement ever since.
17. Her only topic of conversation (*is, are*) her boyfriends.
18. The houses in that new subdivision along the lake (*reminds, remind*) me of Florida.
19. The family upstairs (*starts, start*) yelling at each other before breakfast.
20. The noise of the cows, the crickets, and the birds (*keeps, keep*) me awake.

FILE II: PRACTICE 3. *Be ready to read each of the following sentences aloud, using the verb form in parentheses that agrees with the subject.*

1. Neither Tom nor the twins (*has, have*) any right to complain.
2. Mr. Perkins and his new assistant (*was, were*) helping out.

3. From ten o'clock on, either my brother or my sister (*was*, *were*) using the phone.
4. Too much rain or too much sun (*is*, *are*) bad for those plants.
5. No smoking or spitting (*was*, *were*) allowed on his bus.
6. Arguments about politics or religion always (*upsets*, *upset*) her.
7. Soap and water or vinegar (*cleans*, *clean*) the windows best, I've found.
8. Tom, Dick, or Harry (*is*, *are*) responsible, I'll bet.
9. Neither she nor her friends (*wants*, *want*) to join.
10. Corned beef and cabbage (*is*, *are*) one dish I can't stand.
11. Either the witness or the defendant (*has*, *have*) lied.
12. A former friend and debate partner of Fred's (*was*, *were*) the main speaker at the banquet.
13. Rob or Don (*has*, *have*) an extra ticket, I'm sure.
14. Neither the novel nor the movie (*was*, *were*) especially good.
15. Usually Ann, Pat, or Sally (*brings*, *bring*) her recorder to our practice sessions.
16. Her cousin and best friend (*was*, *were*) her matron of honor.
17. Every time Sharon or Liz (*tries*, *try*) to tell a joke, the punch line gets fouled up.
18. Bread and milk (*was*, *were*) all he got for supper.
19. Neither the cake nor the cookies (*was*, *were*) fresh.
20. Pork and beans (*was*, *were*) the cheapest item on the menu.

FILE II: PRACTICE 4. *Be ready to read each of the following sentences aloud, substituting for the blank the appropriate verb form — either* don't *or* doesn't.

1. It just _____ make sense, does it?
2. The bus _____ stop at that corner.
3. Bert _____ care how much it costs.
4. No, the baby _____ talk yet.
5. That tie _____ look right with that shirt.

6. It _____ seem fair.
7. Jerry _____ look very bright, does he?
8. I wonder why he _____ answer the phone.
9. The paper _____ come till four o'clock.
10. His sarcastic remarks _____ bother me.
11. Dad said it _____ matter.
12. Helen told me she _____ like him.
13. Your dog _____ have fleas, does he?
14. Popcorn _____ make me thirsty.
15. Well, I know it _____ belong to you.
16. Phil and Andy _____ have a chance.
17. I tell you this key _____ fit.
18. Jane likes liver, but Joan _____.
19. This salt shaker _____ work.
20. His boasting _____ impress me.

FILE II: PRACTICE 5. *Be ready to read each of the following sentences aloud, using the verb form in parentheses that agrees with the subject.*

1. Each of the stories (*ends, end*) in a tragedy.
2. Nobody wearing high heels (*is, are*) permitted on the greens.
3. The twins like him, but neither of them (*pays, pay*) any attention to what he says.
4. Everyone on both teams (*agrees, agree*) that the umpire was wrong.
5. Neither of the children (*has, have*) the slightest fear of water.
6. I heard that each of the girls (*was, were*) awarded a prize.
7. I don't think either of the girls (*deserves, deserve*) a prize.
8. Each of the instruments (*is, are*) guaranteed to last a year.
9. Only one of the radios (*works, work*).
10. Everyone buying ten gallons of gas at the Wisco stations (*was, were*) given a raffle ticket.
11. I wonder if either of his brothers (*knows, know*) why he left.

66

12. No, neither of those cars (*belongs, belong*) to us.
13. Each of the children (*has, have*) bright red hair and freckles.
14. No one but Hal and Pete (*wants, want*) to be interviewed.
15. Neither of the girls (*plans, plan*) to go on to school.
16. Every bit of jewelry in the showcases (*was, were*) stolen.
17. However, each of the costumes (*was, were*) OK'd by the director.
18. Neither of my dogs (*likes, like*) to hunt squirrels.
19. No one in any of my study halls (*wastes, waste*) time.
20. Every man, woman, and child in those buildings (*has, have*) already bought a poppy.

FILE II: PRACTICE 6. *Be ready to read each of the following sentences aloud, using the verb form in parentheses that agrees with the subject.*

1. A number of students (*has, have*) signed up already.
2. Andy is the only one of those fellows who (*has, have*) paid his fine.
3. The toad that ate the seven spiders (*was, were*) Jerry's.
4. Benny is one of those people who (*thinks, think*) laws are made for others.
5. Not one of the paintings (*was, were*) damaged in the fire.
6. The number of complaints (*has, have*) finally dwindled.
7. Some letters found in the box with his will (*tells, tell*) the true story.
8. A number of boats (*was, were*) in danger of capsizing.
9. Every torn spot in the nets (*needs, need*) to be mended.
10. The number of boats in the choppy water (*was, were*) surprising.
11. Mr. Firkins or one of the girls (*opens, open*) the shop each day.
12. Uncle Leonard is one of those men who always (*wears, wear*) a tie.
13. Which one of these coats (*belongs, belong*) to Frank?
14. Darrell or the twins (*is, are*) bringing the Pepsis.

15. The number of commercials they squeeze in (*is, are*) appalling, I think.
16. "The Biter Bitten" is the only one of those stories that (*is, are*) worth reading.
17. The main problem (*is, are*) the overcrowded schools.
18. Every one of those fellows now (*has, have*) long sideburns.
19. A bookcase full of paperbacks (*stands, stand*) right inside the door.
20. She is one of those girls who (*looks, look*) good in anything they wear.

FILE II: PRACTICE 7. *Be ready to read each of the following sentences aloud, using the verb form in parentheses that agrees with the subject.*

1. Two thirds of the carpet (*was, were*) badly faded.
2. At least half of the students (*eats, eat*) at the cafeteria.
3. Horseshoes (*was, were*) the favorite game at Willow Haven.
4. He said five dollars and thirty cents (*was, were*) the usual charge.
5. For Billy, even two hours (*is, are*) a long time to wait.
6. Marshall Field and Company now (*has, have*) a branch store here.
7. Three and a half yards (*doesn't, don't*) seem enough for both dresses.
8. *The Invaders* (*is, are*) playing at the Odeon this week.
9. Most of the credit for those reports (*belongs, belong*) to Willa Mae.
10. Fifty miles (*is, are*) quite a distance to hike.
11. Physics (*was, were*) the hardest subject for me.
12. Mrs. Elder says fifteen pounds of spareribs (*is, are*) not enough for her family.
13. Yes, four days (*seems, seem*) a reasonable time for the job.
14. Six pounds (*is, are*) too much weight to gain in a week.
15. Three minutes (*seems, seem*) like three hours when you have to give a three-minute talk in school.

16. But three hours (*seems*, *seem*) like three minutes when you're at a party.
17. Seven tons just (*fills*, *fill*) the bin.
18. Generally mumps (*is*, *are*) milder than measles.
19. Half of this piece with the pecans and raisins (*is*, *are*) enough for me.
20. Thirty-two cubic feet of water (*weighs*, *weigh*) nearly a ton.

FILE II: PRACTICE 8.   *Be ready to read each of the following sentences aloud, using the verb form in parentheses that agrees with the subject.*

1. Here (*comes*, *come*) the twins.
2. There (*goes*, *go*) the Good Humor trucks back to the garage to reload.
3. (*Where's*, *Where are*) the Christmas cards I ordered?
4. (*There's*, *There are*) still a few copies left.
5. (*Was*, *Were*) the gun or the missing diary ever found?
6. (*Does*, *Do*) either of you boys have a match?
7. (*Has*, *Have*) the rest of the names been checked?
8. Here (*goes*, *go*) my last two nickels.
9. Where (*was*, *were*) your parents last night?
10. Hidden in the mattress (*was*, *were*) three diamond rings and one hundred ten-dollar bills.
11. (*Wasn't*, *Weren't*) Mom and Dad with you the first time you drove?
12. There (*isn't*, *aren't*) enough potato chips.
13. (*How's*, *How are*) all your aches and pains?
14. Here (*comes*, *come*) my aunt and uncle.
15. (*Isn't*, *Aren't*) there any messages for me?
16. In yesterday's paper there (*was*, *were*) two ads for a busboy.
17. And there—right where he had left them—(*was*, *were*) his keys.
18. (*Here's*, *Here are*) the balloons for the party.
19. (*Isn't*, *Aren't*) there some nails and a hammer in the toolbox?
20. There once (*was*, *were*) forty errors made in a single game!

FILE II: PRACTICE 9. *Be ready to read each of the following sentences aloud, substituting for each blank the appropriate verb form — either* was *or* were.

1. You _____ wrong again, _____n't you?
2. Where _____ the sheriff and his men?
3. And where _____ you last night?
4. You _____ n't home, _____ you?
5. We _____ working while you _____ loafing.
6. When _____ you notified?
7. _____ your brothers at school?
8. You _____ going to Sharon's, _____n't you?
9. What _____ you complaining about?
10. He _____ really scared, I tell you.
11. How _____ they supposed to know you _____ there?
12. You _____n't kidding me, _____ you?
13. They _____n't invited, _____ they?
14. You _____n't really surprised, _____ you?
15. _____ you at the picnic?
16. No, we _____ at the movies.
17. What _____ you doing in the principal's office?
18. You _____ supposed to go right home, _____n't you?
19. We _____ robbed!
20. The tickets _____n't yours; they _____ mine.

FILE II: PRACTICE 10. A RE-DRILL. *Be ready to read each of the following sentences aloud, using the verb form in parentheses that agrees with the subject.*

1. (*Doesn't, Don't*) that cake smell good?
2. Every one of the peaches (*was, were*) wormy.
3. (*Is, Are*) your mother or father in, Eddie?
4. That box of Jerry's old toys (*belongs, belong*) in the attic.
5. No, it (*doesn't, don't*) seem so funny today.
6. Either the manager or the coach (*is, are*) always yelling at the umpire.

7. We (*was, were*) fit to be tied, I can tell you.
8. Dad (*doesn't, don't*) get up before noon on Saturdays.
9. There (*goes, go*) those stuck-up Lorrimer twins.
10. Twenty-five minutes of advertising (*is, are*) too much.
11. (*Has, Have*) the mailman and the milkman been here yet?
12. (*Here's, Here are*) those tickets I promised you.
13. (*Where's, Where are*) Dad's keys?
14. (*Isn't, Aren't*) there enough chairs for everyone?
15. Here (*comes, come*) the cheerleaders now.
16. Neither the roast nor the potatoes (*is, are*) done yet.
17. Every one of those telephone booths (*was, were*) in use.
18. The plaster on both these ceilings (*has, have*) cracked.
19. Either rain or snow (*is, are*) expected this evening.
20. The manager, as well as his assistant, (*has, have*) agreed to attend.

FILE II: PRACTICE 11. A RE-DRILL. *Be ready to read each of the following sentences aloud, using the verb form in parentheses that agrees with the subject.*

1. Here (*comes, come*) my best friend and bitterest rival, Tim Polk.
2. Hidden under the blotter (*was, were*) the two photographs I was looking for.
3. Why (*doesn't, don't*) someone answer the doorbell?
4. Where (*was, were*) Andy and Joel?
5. (*Has, Have*) Mr. Theisen or his assistant arrived yet?
6. You (*was, were*) wrong, and they (*was, were*) wrong too.
7. (*Doesn't, Don't*) he work at Harry's Grill now?
8. The last number on the program (*was, were*) several short violin selections by Jack Benny.
9. "Thirteen Ways to Improve Your Looks" (*is, are*) in the Easter issue.
10. Mrs. Penrod, like her husband, (*likes, like*) peace and quiet.
11. Neither his story nor mine (*was, were*) accepted.
12. His main problem (*was, were*) the constant interruptions.

13. The verb in those sentences, as well as the subject, (*has, have*) to be plural.
14. His suggestions for improving the service in the cafeteria (*was, were*) excellent.
15. No person or persons (*is, are*) going to stop him.
16. The butter in these sandwiches (*tastes, taste*) rancid.
17. Measles sometimes (*leaves, leave*) serious aftereffects.
18. Why (*doesn't, don't*) your uncle call the FBI?
19. Neither of the movies (*sounds, sound*) good.
20. Then why (*doesn't, don't*) that bunch of flowers make him sneeze?

FILE II: PRACTICE 12. A RE-DRILL. *Be ready to read each of the following sentences aloud, using the verb form in parentheses that agrees with the subject.*

1. You (*was, were*) a football coach once, (*wasn't, weren't*) you, Mr. Lenz?
2. (*Was, Were*) that you who won the lottery?
3. Yes, and we (*was, were*) absolutely flabbergasted.
4. Dominoes (*isn't, aren't*) such a hard game to learn.
5. Weeden, Fencil, and Company (*does, do*) most of our ads.
6. That navy skirt with the box pleats (*is, are*) the best buy.
7. One of the goals (*was, were*) made by Bobby Hull.
8. Joanie, like her brothers, (*is, are*) a topnotch swimmer.
9. (*Doesn't, Don't*) he know that money (*doesn't, don't*) grow on trees?
10. Every one of those recipes (*calls, call*) for a cup of butter.
11. (*There's, There are*) your uncle and aunt now.
12. Neither the rolls nor the bread (*was, were*) fresh.
13. Everybody from both towns always (*turns, turn*) up for this game.
14. (*There's, There are*) two more sandwiches in the refrigerator.
15. Don't you think that six dollars and ninety-eight cents (*is, are*) too much to pay for that tie?
16. Boom (*goes, go*) the cannons!

17. Each of the contestants (*was*, *were*) asked the same five questions.
18. There (*was*, *were*) at least sixty men in the line when I got there.
19. (*Is*, *Are*) Les Perri or Bill Tate on the team?
20. (*Does*, *Do*) either of these letters weigh more than an ounce?

FILE II: PRACTICE 13.   A RE-DRILL.   *Be ready to read each of the following sentences aloud, using the verb form in parentheses that agrees with the subject.*

1. Nobody, not even the students, (*wants*, *want*) another tournament.
2. *The Merry Wives of Windsor* (*is*, *are*) to be presented next.
3. My favorite dessert (*is*, *are*) chocolate parfaits; their favorite (*is*, *are*) brownies.
4. Arguments about politics or religion (*annoys*, *annoy*) my aunt, but neither of the guests (*was*, *were*) aware of this.
5. Meyers, Bell, or Slotkin (*is*, *are*) going to pitch.
6. Just one of the officials at these business-league games (*gets*, *get*) paid.
7. A long line of pickets (*surrounds*, *surround*) the plant this morning.
8. (*Has*, *Have*) either of your neighbors ever complained about your parking the car in the alley?
9. The only guide they had on these trips (*was*, *were*) the stars.
10. His brothers, as well as his dad, (*was*, *were*) proud of him.
11. (*There's*, *There are*) at least six overdue library books under his bed, I'll bet.
12. Their survey showed that one out of every four doctors (*recommends*, *recommend*) Slim-slo.
13. (*Does*, *Do*) either of your parents attend the P.T.A. meetings?
14. Usually Ted or one of the Martin twins (*takes*, *take*) care of the ticket money.
15. (*Wasn't*, *Weren't*) both of the men on that route given the same instructions?

FILE DRAWER 3

pronoun
usage

between you and me

When some people were growing up, they were frequently reminded, or they heard others reminded, that a nominative pronoun form (*she, I, they*), not an objective form (*her, me, them*), should be used in sentences like "You and she should stay"; "Sam and I will go"; "It was they." In fact, these people heard the nominative forms stressed so much that after a while phrases like "you and her" and "Sam and me" came to sound "wrong" to them almost anywhere in a sentence. As a result, such people will say "between you and she" and "between Sam and I."

But *between* is a preposition, and in standard English objective pronoun forms are the correct forms to use as objects of prepositions: *between you and* **me**, *between you and* **her**, *between you and* **him**, *between you and* **us**, *between you and* **them**.

DOUBLE SUBJECTS

Is the boldfaced pronoun in each of the following sentences necessary?

A buddy of mine **he** used to work in a glue factory.

My oldest sister **she** lives in Detroit now.

The answer is, of course, obvious. Since each sentence has a subject noun—*buddy* and *sister*—there is no need for the pronoun. It adds nothing to the meaning of the sentence. About the only thing it does is make the sentence sound rather childish. Notice how much more adult-sounding the sentences are without the pronouns:

A buddy of mine used to work in a glue factory.

My oldest sister lives in Detroit now.

"HISSELF" AND COMPANY

Look at the following list of "self" pronouns, noticing particularly the letters printed in boldface type. Compare these boldfaced forms with the italicized words opposite them.

SINGULAR:	**my**self	*my* birthday
	yourself	*your* prize
	himself	*his* work
	herself	*her* time
	itself	*its* beak
PLURAL:	**our**selves	*our* efforts
	yourselves	*your* tickets
	themselves	*their* plans

These "self" pronouns are another good example of the fact that language is not always logical. Since users of standard English say *"my*self" and *"your*self" and *"her*self," you would expect that they would also say *"his*self" and *"their*selves." But they don't. *Hisself* and *theirselves*—though logical—are used only in nonstandard English. Someday these nonstandard forms might become acceptable. But until they do, avoid them. Avoid also the not-so-logical forms *ourselfs, ourself, theirself.*

He behaved **himself** after that.   [Not: *hisself.*]

Ma told us to help **ourselves.**   [Not: *ourselfs* or *ourself.*]

The boys did all the work **themselves.**   [Not: *theirselves* or *theirself.*]

It's me (him, her, us, them)

In answer to the question "Who is it?" or "Who's there?" you might give your name: "Charles" or "It's Alice." But what if you use a pronoun? Should you say "It's *me*" or "It is *I*"?

According to the rules of formal grammar, the various forms of the linking verb *be* should be followed by nominative pronoun forms: It is *I*; It was *I*; It was *he*; and so on. But *It's me* (once considered nonstandard) has been so widely used by educated people everywhere that it is now standard usage, even though some users of formal English still prefer *It is I*, especially in writing.

But though *It's me* is now fully accepted, *It's him*, *It's her*, *It's us*, *It's them* are not.

myself

The pronoun *myself* is most frequently used as either a reflexive or an intensive. As a reflexive pronoun, it is used as the object of a verb or a preposition in a sentence whose subject is *I*:

I congratulated myself.   [Direct object.]

I gave myself quite a scare.   [Indirect object.]

I was annoyed with myself.   [Object of preposition.]

As an intensive pronoun, *myself* is used for emphasis:

I myself can't see the difference.

I did not see the accident myself.

Note: The usage facts above apply as well to other "self" pronouns—*yourself*, *himself*, *herself*, etc.

In colloquial English *myself* is sometimes used instead of *I* as the second part of a compound subject. But this usage is avoided in writing:

COLLOQUIAL: Audrey and myself discovered the fire.
WRITTEN: Audrey and I discovered the fire.

More common, in informal English anyway, is the use of *myself* instead of *me* as the second part of the compound object of a verb or a preposition:

Alice told only Ralph and myself.

Uncle Ben gave my sister and myself first choice.

Later the bus driver apologized to Cleo and myself.

But even though this usage appears in both speech and writing, most people avoid it and use *me* instead:

Alice told only Ralph and me.

Uncle Ben gave my sister and me first choice.

Later the bus driver apologized to Cleo and me.

NOMINATIVE AND OBJECTIVE PRONOUN FORMS

In standard English, different pronoun forms are used to do different jobs in sentences. For example, when a personal pronoun is used as the subject of a sentence, one of these *nominative* forms is used:

NOMINATIVE FORMS: I, you, he, she, it; we, you, they

When a personal pronoun is used as a direct or indirect object or as the object of a preposition, one of these *objective* forms is used:

OBJECTIVE FORMS: me, you, him, her, it; us, you, them

In sentences where a pronoun is used *by itself* as the subject or as an object, almost everyone, without giving it any

80

thought, uses a standard form. Consider these sentences, for example:

I closed all the windows.   [Nominative form; subject of the sentence.]

Allan saw **her** standing in the wings.   [Objective form; direct object.]

The Blaneys paid no attention to **him**.   [Objective form; object of preposition *to*.]

However, it is quite a different matter when it comes to sentences in which a pronoun is not used by itself but is paired with a noun or another pronoun in a compound subject or object. Then all too often people will say:

NONSTANDARD: *Perry and* **me** closed all the windows.

NONSTANDARD: Allan saw *Otto and* **she** standing in the wings.

NONSTANDARD: The Blaneys paid no attention to **he** *and* **I**.

Do you ever use nonstandard forms like these? Find out, by putting your ear to work. Listen to the pronoun forms you use in compound subjects and objects, and test the forms like this: Say the sentence, dropping one part of the compound subject. Since you always use the right form when you use a pronoun alone, your ear will tell you immediately that *I*, not *me*, is the form that should be used in this sentence:

[Perry and] **I** closed all the windows.

As you can see, trying a pronoun out by itself in a sentence provides a pretty foolproof way to determine not only whether you

81

are using a nonstandard form but also what the standard form is.

Try the "ear test" on the other two nonstandard sentences. Notice that if you read the sentences without the words in brackets, you cannot help getting the right form of the pronoun:

Allan saw [Otto and] **her** standing in the wings.

The Blaneys paid no attention to **him** [and I].

The Blaneys paid no attention to [him and] **me**.

Two special problems are pronouns used as appositives and in short answers to questions. A pronoun appositive may be either nominative or objective, depending on what work the word it explains does in the sentence. For example:

The two finalists, Catherine and **he**, received transistor radios.   [Not: *him*. The pronoun should be a nominative form because it is in apposition with the subject *finalists*.]

Transistor radios were presented to the two finalists, Catherine and **him**.   [Not: *he*. The pronoun should be an objective form because it is in apposition with *finalists*, the object of the preposition *to*.]

Sometimes in deciding whether to use a nominative or an objective form in the answer to a question, you may need to supply mentally words that you would not actually say:

"Did the nurse notify anyone?" "Yes, Gladys and **me**."   [Not: *I*. The meaning is "The nurse notified Gladys and me."]

"Didn't anyone offer to help?" "Only John and **he**."   [Not: *him*. The meaning is "Only John and he offered to help."]

"Who broke the window?" "Not **I**."   [Not: *me*. The meaning is "It was not I who broke the window."]

In casual conversation, the objective form is often used in sentences like the last two ("Didn't anyone offer to help?" "Only John and him"; "Who broke the window?" "Not me"), perhaps because the pronoun comes at the end of the sentence, in object territory. But the objective form would not be appropriate in writing or in careful speech.

ORDER OF PRONOUNS

As a courtesy, users of standard English refer to themselves *after* they have referred to someone else:

> Only **Rocco** and **I** could understand him.   [Not: Only *I* and *Rocco*.]

> In the end she hired both **them** and **us**.   [Not: *us* and *them*.]

> They are depending on **you** and **me**.   [Not: *me* and *you*.]

POSSESSIVE FORMS

In writing, an apostrophe is used with nouns that indicate possession:

Len's boat	the puppy's tail	a woman's voice
the Otts' car	all voters' names	the men's jobs

No apostrophe should be used, however, with the possessive pronouns *yours, his, hers, its, ours, theirs, whose*, or with the possessive adjectives *his, its, whose*. In any writing you do, check to see that you have not put an apostrophe in these pronoun and adjective forms that show ownership *without* an apostrophe:

I wish I had a memory like **yours**.   [Not: *your's*.]

We sold **ours** last week.   [Not: *our's*.]

Its wing was broken.   [Not: *It's*, which is the contraction of *It is*.]

Whose turn was it?   [Not: *Who's*, which is the contraction of *Who is*.]

PRONOUN AGREEMENT: IN NUMBER

A pronoun generally agrees with its antecedent (the word it refers to) in number. This means that if the antecedent is singular, singular pronouns are used to refer to it. If the antecedent is plural, plural pronouns are used to refer to it. For example:

The *doctor* couldn't remember where **he** had laid **his** stethoscope.

The *doctors* said that **they** had lowered **their** fees.

If all sentences were like these, there would be few, if any, problems in pronoun agreement. It is hard to imagine anyone making a mistake in such sentences. But there are some sentences that do seem to trigger mistakes — sentences like these:

PEOPLE SAY:

Before a *person* signs a contract, **they** ought to read it.

If an *employee* is going to be late, **they** should call and tell **their** supervisor.

Before a *person* signs a contract, **he** ought to read it.

If an *employee* is going to be late, **he** should call and tell **his** supervisor.

What causes the mismatching in such sentences is probably that although the speaker says "a person" or "an employee," he is not thinking of one particular person or employee. He has in mind any one or more of a whole group of people. And this "plural" idea in his mind leads him to use a plural pronoun form. A plural form may seem sensible, but since the words *person* and *employee* are singular, a singular form should be used, especially in writing.

PRONOUN AGREEMENT: IN PERSON

A pronoun should agree with its antecedent in person (as well as in number).* This means, for example, that the pronoun *you* should not be used to refer to an antecedent in the third person, as in the following sentence:

If a *student* wants to drop a course, **you** have to get **your** counselor's permission.

Since the antecedent *student* is in the third person, the third-person forms *he* and *his* should be used instead of *you* and *your*:

If a *student* wants to drop a course, **he** has to get **his** counselor's permission.

---

*Personal pronouns are divided into three groups—
First person, the one speaking: *I, we*
Second person, the one spoken to: *you*
Third person, the one spoken of: *he, she, it, they*
Nouns and indefinites are regarded as third person.

Or—in some circumstances—*you* could be substituted for *student*:

> If **you** want to drop a course, *you* have to get *your* counselor's permission.

PRONOUN AGREEMENT: WITH INDEFINITES

The "indefinites"—words like *anybody, anyone, everybody, everyone, somebody, someone, nobody, no one, one, each, either, neither* —are singular, as you can tell from the fact that singular verbs are used with them:

> Then each *takes* a turn.

> Neither *looks* right.

> *Was* anyone in the pool at the time?

When personal pronouns are used to refer to these indefinites, the pronouns should, as a rule, be singular also:

> Of course *each* of the women thought **she** had the answer.

> *Neither* of the boys had stopped to change **his** clothes before **he** left.

> If *anyone* objects, tell **him** to see Mrs. Foster.

In conversation plural forms are often used, especially in sentences like the last, in which the "anyone" could be a woman as well as a man. In fact, some people, promoters of women's rights among them, would prefer the plural form *them* to the masculine singular *him* (or the clumsy phrase *him or her*) in a sentence like this.

But common as the plural is in speech, it is not considered appropriate in writing:

SPOKEN: Everyone gave what they could.
WRITTEN: Everyone gave what he could.

In some sentences the indefinite is so clearly plural in meaning that it would sound ridiculous to use a singular pronoun with it. For example:

Everyone in the club must have enjoyed the program, because **he** stayed until the very end.

There are two ways of handling this problem. In informal English, the plural pronoun would be used, even though it does not agree with the antecedent:

Everyone in the club must have enjoyed the program, because **they** stayed until the very end.

In formal English, however, the sentence would be rephrased so that the agreement rule would not be broken:

All the club *members* must have enjoyed the program, because **they** stayed until the very end.

PRONOUNS AND NOUNS WITH GERUNDS

A pronoun or a proper noun immediately preceding a gerund (an *-ing* verb form used as a noun) is usually in the possessive:

They didn't seem to mind **my** watching them work.

Your challenging Peter to a duel was rather ridiculous.

Why should they object to **our** selling the store?

Sandy was flustered by **their** needling.

I was surprised at **his** quitting the team.

She was upset about **John's** leaving home.

When a common noun directly precedes a gerund, usage is divided. In formal English, the possessive form is usual; in informal English, the ordinary form is often used:

> FORMAL: She was unhappy about her **son's** moving so far away.
> INFORMAL: She was unhappy about her **son** moving so far away.

The ordinary form is generally used for plural nouns:

> My grandfather disapproves of **women** working outside the home.

> She hadn't heard about the **twins** being suspended.

When emphasis is wanted for the noun or pronoun, rather than for the gerund that names the action, the ordinary form of the noun and the objective form of the pronoun are used:

> I was surprised at **Gerald** quitting the team.

> I was surprised at **him** quitting the team.

In speech the words *Gerald* and *him* would be stressed.

PRONOUNS AS PREDICATE COMPLEMENTS

Each of the following sentences contains a form of the linking verb *be* followed by a predicate complement. Notice that the predicate complement refers to the same person or thing as the subject:

He *will be* the lead-off *batter.*   [Batter = He.]

Chuck and she *should have been* the *winners.*
[Winners = Chuck and she.]

They *must have been* the mysterious *callers.*   [Callers = They.]

Now suppose that each of these sentences is rewritten so that the predicate complement becomes the subject. Since the complements and the subjects refer to the same people, they can be switched around without changing the meaning of the sentences:

The lead-off batter will be **he**.

The winners should have been **Chuck and she.**

The mysterious callers must have been **they.**

Notice that the pronouns—now used as predicate complements—are nominative forms, just as they were when they were used as subjects.

In standard English, especially in writing and careful speech, the nominative form is used for pronoun predicate complements:

Someone in the office started the rumor; I suspect it was **she**.

It wasn't **we** who suggested leaving.

The only ones who objected to the plan were **he** and his brother.

But in casual conversation you will often hear the objective form of the pronoun:

> Someone in the office started the rumor; I suspect it was **her**.

Sometimes people feel that the nominative form sounds too formal, and the objective form too informal. Then they usually solve the problem by rephrasing:

> Someone in the office started the rumor; I suspect she was the one.

PRONOUNS IN COMPARISONS

You would seldom hear or read sentences like these:

> Jane can change a tire faster than he can change a tire.

> Rodney will be as glad as I am glad.

The sentences sound rather strange because they include more words than would generally be used in comparing one thing with another. Most people would omit the words following *he* and *I*, since the meaning of the sentences would be perfectly clear without them:

> Jane can change a tire faster than **he** [can change a tire].

> Rodney will be as glad as **I** [am glad].

Although the words in brackets are not important enough, as far as the meaning goes, to be expressed, they are important for another reason: They serve as a clue to tell you what form of the pronoun should be used after a word like *than* or *as*. For example, the "understood" words in brackets in the following sentences show that the pronouns should be *nominative* forms because each is the subject of the unexpressed verb:

> Do you know anyone who works more slowly than **she** [works]?

> They play a more professional game than **we** [play].

> We don't win as often as **they** [do].

The "understood" words in the next three sentences show that the pronouns should be *objective* forms because each is used as an object:

> Her brother sent me twice as many postcards as [he sent] **her**.

> Since Harry had done harder work, Mrs. Vito paid him two dollars more than [she paid] **us**.

> She doesn't think it will take her as long as [it took] **them**.

In some sentences either a nominative or an objective pronoun might be used, depending on the meaning intended:

> I don't miss Clara as much as **he** [misses Clara].

> I don't miss Clara as much as [I miss] **him**.

In sentences like these especially, you can see how important it is to use the right form of the pronoun. Unless you do, your intended meaning may be misunderstood.

In informal speech, objective forms are sometimes used (instead of nominative forms) in sentences like "She's two years older than *me*" and "I'm taller than *him*." But these forms are generally avoided in writing and in formal speech.

them, those, they

Speakers of nonstandard English sometimes use the pronoun *them* as the subject of a sentence:

NONSTANDARD: **Them** can't be Bruce's skates.

NONSTANDARD: **Them** are too small.

NONSTANDARD: **Them** on the stairs are probably his.

But in standard English the form *them* is used only as an object:

Don't put any radishes on my plate. I don't like **them.**

Jane and Lucy like radishes. Take some for **them.**

If the boys call, tell **them** the news.

As a speaker of standard English, you should use one of the following forms — not *them* — in the subject position:

STANDARD: **Those** can't be Bruce's skates.

STANDARD: **They** are too small.

STANDARD: **The ones** on the stairs are probably his.

we [boys], us [boys]

Which should you say: "Mr. Garvey held *we boys* responsible" or "Mr. Garvey held *us boys* responsible"? Which should you say: "Only *we boys* were allowed to drive the tractor" or "Only *us boys* were allowed to drive the tractor"?

Deciding whether to use *we* or *us* in sentences like these is easy. Just determine which pronoun forms you would use if

92

the word *boys* were not in the sentences. Those are the forms you should use:

> Mr. Garvey held **us** [boys] responsible.

> Only **we** [boys] were allowed to drive the tractor.

> Their silly excuses didn't fool **us** [girls] for a minute.

> She used to call on everyone but **us** [two].

who, which, that, whose

In standard English the relative pronoun *who* is most commonly used to refer to people. It is also used to refer to animals, especially when they are thought of as having personalities:

> We took our ailing plant to Mr. Kelso, who writes a gardening column for the local newspaper.

> Do you know anyone who plays the sitar?

> Next I was introduced to Lancelot, who immediately offered me his paw to shake.

The relative pronoun *which* is used to refer to things (including animals):

> The Brand X Company, which went bankrupt last year, may soon be back in business under a new name.

> Goff was always telling long, involved stories which no one could follow.

> They were sent out to rescue a dolphin which had gotten stranded on the beach.

That is used to refer to people or things:

> He is not the guide that the Klines recommended.

> Have you read the reply that Gordon wrote?

When a relative pronoun referring to a person shows possession, *whose* is used:

> In his next movie he plays a cavalry officer whose troops are massacred because of his negligence.

> Imogene, whose advice I seldom ignore, had warned me not to volunteer.

When the relative refers to a thing rather than a person, *whose* or the more formal—and more clumsy—*of which* is used:

> Behind the house was a weather-beaten barn, whose roof had fallen in.   [Or: . . . the roof of which had fallen in.]

who, whom

How do you decide whether the nominative form *who* or the objective form *whom* is the one needed in a sentence? It is not hard. Just figure out how the pronoun is being used.

If the pronoun is being used as the subject of a sentence or clause or as a predicate complement, the nominative form *who* (or its compound *whoever*) is the form you need:

> **Who** drew the mustache on her picture?   [Subject of verb *drew*.]

> They didn't announce **who** came in third.   [Subject of verb *came* in noun clause *who came in third*.]

Give **whoever** delivers the flowers a tip.   [Subject of verb *delivers* in noun clause *whoever delivers the flowers.*]

We never learned **who** the masked man was.   [Predicate complement in noun clause *who the masked man was.*]

If the pronoun is being used as a direct object or object of a preposition, the objective form *whom* (or its compound *whomever*) is the form you need:

Whom does Winslow suspect?   [Object of verb *does suspect.*]

They usually elect **whomever** Ed suggests.   [Object of verb *suggests* in noun clause *whomever Ed suggests.*]

Whom were you working with that day?   [Object of preposition *with.*]

In informal English, *who* is frequently used at the beginning of a sentence—in subject territory—even when the pronoun is the object of a verb or preposition:

Who does Winslow suspect?

Who were you working with that day?

But when a preposition comes immediately before the pronoun, both formal and informal English use *whom*:

With **whom** were you working that day?

For **whom** was the letter intended?

Suggestion: In figuring out how the pronoun is used in a clause, you will find it helpful to separate the clause from the rest of the sentence. In the following sentence, for example, the pronoun *whoever* might at first glance seem to be the object of the preposition *to*:

> Give the tickets to whoever wants them.

But if you separate the clause from the rest of the sentence, you will see immediately that the whole clause is the object of the preposition *to* and that *in the clause* the pronoun *whoever* is the subject of the verb *wants*:

> Give the tickets to [whoever wants them].

A little trickier are sentences in which an interrupting expression like *I thought* or *he believes* or *does she think* follows the pronoun. These expressions should be ignored in determining which form to use:

> SENTENCE: I called several people who I thought might give me a ride.
> CLAUSE: who [I thought] might give me a ride

Once you drop the expression *I thought*, you can see that the pronoun *who* is the subject of the verb *might give*, not the object of the verb *thought*.

FILE III: PRACTICE 1.   *Be ready to read each of the following sentences aloud, using the pronoun form in parentheses appropriate in standard English.*

1. Steve and (*she, her*) are going steady.
2. The Olsons invited Peter and (*I, me*) to supper.

3. (*He, Him*) and (*I, me*) made the second team.
4. Everyone but Liz and (*I, me*) got the joke.
5. Between you and (*I, me*), I can't stand Benny.
6. Why didn't Gordon and (*she, her*) give you and (*I, me*) their tickets?
7. My guess is that Nora and (*he, him*) will go by train.
8. Neither (*he, him*) nor (*she, her*) likes flying.
9. Who do Ted and (*she, her*) think they are?
10. Harry and (*I, me*) started running toward the garage.
11. Rob and (*I, me*) gave our copies to Larry and (*she, her*).
12. Dan said that Bonnie and (*she, her*) already had dates.
13. Dan saw Bonnie and (*she, her*) last night at the carnival.
14. Couldn't you and (*he, him*) have waited for Ellen and (*I, me*)?
15. Before long (*he, him*) and (*she, her*) were snarling at each other.
16. For Ron and (*I, me*) she had brought two handwoven ponchos.
17. He gave Kurt and (*she, her*) each a quarter.
18. Everyone signed the gift card except Jean and (*he, him*).
19. Aunt Elsie said that (*he, him*) and (*she, her*) hated picnics.
20. Mrs. Valdez offered Tim and (*she, her*) a ride to school.

FILE III: PRACTICE 2. *Be ready to read the following sentences aloud, substituting the appropriate form—I or me—for each blank.*

1. Gary interviewed Philip and _____.
2. Then Philip and _____ interviewed Gary.
3. The manager told my cousin and _____ to put our bikes in the back.
4. Between you and _____, he's a rat.
5. To Dan and _____, most of the skits seemed real corn.
6. No, Clem didn't beat Joe and _____; Joe and _____ beat Clem.
7. We can't lose—with Andy and _____ on the team.

8. I thought she intended the cake for Pat and _____.
9. Hank wants to know if he can go over with you and _____.
10. Just between you and _____, you and _____ were wrong again.
11. Alice Kay passed the secret on to Fred and _____.
12. Either you or _____ should pay for the damage.
13. Luckily Mr. Morgan had offered Pete and _____ a part-time job.
14. Without Otis and _____, they'll never make it.
15. Behind Sam and _____ stood that pesty Gus Miller.
16. If Bert and _____ had had our way, either Bert or _____ would have been the emcee.
17. As for Ozzie and _____, we couldn't stand her.
18. Uncle Neil watched over Sue and _____ like a hawk.
19. They wanted to go bowling, and so did Chris and _____.
20. I hope you will vote for Ken and _____.

FILE III: PRACTICE 3. *Be ready to read each of the following sentences aloud, using the pronoun form in parentheses appropriate in standard English.*

1. It wasn't Harold who hit me; it was (*she, her*).
2. I still think it was (*he, him*).
3. The only ones who can type are you and (*I, me*).
4. If it wasn't (*he, him*) who told on us, it must have been (*she, her*).
5. Is that (*she, her*) talking to the cashier?
6. No, that can't be (*she, her*); that woman is much too tall.
7. Are you sure it was (*he, him*) who waited on you and (*I, me*)?
8. If I were (*he, him*), I'd give up.
9. Was it you or (*she, her*) who turned in the alarm?
10. It was (*she, her*); I just got here.
11. Could that be (*they, them*) at the next table?
12. The only ones who haven't paid are (*he, him*) and (*she, her*).

13. The best chess players at our school now are Ross and (*I, me*).
14. And then it was (*we, us*) who had to clean up the place.
15. Why is it always (*he, him*) who gets stuck with the check?
16. But it was (*I, me*) who paid yesterday and the day before.
17. Wasn't it (*they, them*) who wanted to go there in the first place?
18. This ought to be (*she, her*) coming up the stairs now.
19. He finally admitted it was (*he, him*) driving the red car.
20. Thank goodness, it wasn't (*they, them*) who wrecked the car.

FILE III: PRACTICE 4.   *Be ready to read each of the following sentences aloud, using the pronoun form in parentheses appropriate in standard English.*

1. No, I can't run as fast as (*he, him*).
2. But he can't swim as well as (*I, me*).
3. They were just as guilty as (*we, us*).
4. If Jennie and you did the same amount of work, why should he pay you more than (*she, her*)?
5. I don't know; I just felt I should have been paid more than (*she, her*).
6. The green coat fits you better than (*I, me*), don't you think?
7. The waiter charged me more than (*she, her*), though (*she and I, me and her*) had exactly the same meal.
8. He suspected Bob as well as (*I, me*) and watched every move we made.
9. They didn't make as many runs as (*we, us*).
10. I despised Ben as much as (*she, her*), though she had less reason to dislike him than (*I, me*).
11. It was more fun to tease him than (*she, her*).
12. Mr. Clancy trusts Sara more than (*I, me*); I know her much better than (*he, him*).
13. As a matter of fact, Dave hit Rob even harder than (*I, me*), so why should I get all the blame?
14. Sally bet she could hold her breath longer than (*he, him*).

15. Oh, Dad is the problem; it will be easier to persuade Mother than (*he, him*).
16. Marty is taller than (*I, me*), but I weigh more than (*he, him*).
17. Yes; moreover the Lerners are richer than (*they, them*).
18. It's better to ask her for the money than (*he, him*).
19. I despised Ben as much as (*she, her*), so I avoided them both.
20. After all, you didn't have to walk as far as (*we, us*).

FILE III: PRACTICE 5. *Be ready to read each of the following sentences aloud, using the pronoun form in parentheses appropriate in standard English.*

1. Most of (*we, us*) seniors wouldn't sign the petition.
2. Why must (*we, us*) two always do the hard jobs?
3. I still don't see why (*them, those*) won't do.
4. In fact, my brother and (*myself, I, me*) were both invited.
5. Why didn't you buy (*them, the ones*) with the vinyl trim?
6. No, (*them, those*) are mine.
7. Ann had copies made for both (*me and you, you and me*).
8. I'd tell Larry to ask her (*himself, hisself*).
9. After all, it was (*we, us*) girls who thought up the idea.
10. The watchman told (*we, us*) fellows to get out and stay out.
11. (*Them, Those*) are the ones I would buy.
12. (*We, Us*) men stayed home and watched the game.
13. Uncle Ken told (*we, us*) two that we'd have to pay for the damage.
14. Are (*them, those*) the socks you knitted?
15. Did you expect (*we, us*) fellows to pay for all the tickets?
16. Dad said so (*himself, hisself*), didn't he?
17. What made her think that (*we, us*) two had eaten the whole box?
18. I was mad because Mrs. Hilton had praised Ellen more than (*myself, I, me*).
19. Mom thinks (*them, those*) are too expensive.
20. He warned both (*me and Al, Al and me*) to stay away.

FILE III: PRACTICE 6.   *Be ready to read each of the following sentences aloud, using the pronoun form in parentheses appropriate in standard English.*

1. The dance committee—Blake, Rita, and (*I, me*)—met in Room 222.
2. (*Me and Ken, Ken and I*) were both sent to the dean's office.
3. Why were you and (*he, him*) hanging around Dave's locker?
4. Hank couldn't have seen either of us—Bob or (*I, me*).
5. The Steins and (*we, us*) are going in their car.
6. Everyone except Roy and (*he, him*) contributed a quarter.
7. But it wasn't (*I, me*) who dented your fender.
8. His brother isn't as conceited as (*he, him*).
9. Phil, who is much taller than (*I, me*), couldn't even reach the shelf.
10. Dad gave my little brother a bigger helping than (*I, me*).
11. What were you and (*they, them*) whispering about?
12. Actually, the boots fit her better than (*I, me*).
13. Well, the only ones who can play chess are Bobby and (*she, her*).
14. What makes you think it was (*he, him*) who called?
15. Jerry is always tagging after Chris and (*I, me*).
16. The Petris and (*they, them*) are going on the bus.
17. The two worst players, Jim and (*I, me*), each won a prize!
18. Phil feels slighted because Miss Karl praised Wally more than (*he, him*).
19. My mother won't let me invite either Pat or (*she, her*).
20. We eat dinner an hour earlier than (*they, them*).

FILE III: PRACTICE 7.   *Each of the following sentences has one or more nonstandard pronoun forms. Be ready to read the sentences aloud, substituting standard forms for the nonstandard ones.*

1. Pete brought enough pizza for Al and she and we three.
2. Them aren't yours; them are the ones he bought for hisself.
3. Tom's dad hisself had come over in the truck.

4. Them on the top belong to Frank and I.
5. Are them the magazines you and him wanted?
6. Then Cal and me ended by doing all the work ourself.
7. From then on Joe and him behaved theirself.
8. Nobody hates homework as much as me and him.
9. Why don't you ask Gordon and he? They know the way better than me.
10. Why should me and him do all that work for nothing?
11. You diving off that board really impressed Sadie and I.
12. Us girls think it was him who took the letter.
13. As it turned out, Lori and her just outsmarted theirself.
14. Dad made Ralph and I apologize.
15. The only ones who signed up were us two and him.
16. Me letting him copy my theme got both we fellows in a lot of trouble.
17. By this time me and him were worried.
18. Where did you and them go for hamburgers?
19. Us girls will speak for ourself.
20. Luckily me and her could run faster than them.

FILE III: PRACTICE 8.   *Be ready to read each of the following sentences aloud, using the pronoun form in parentheses that agrees with its antecedent.*

1. Once a friend makes a promise, (*he, they*) should keep it.
2. Neither of the women was willing to express (*her, their*) opinion.
3. You ought to know a person well before you lend (*him, them*) money.
4. Before a customer complains, (*he, they*) should make sure the mistake was not (*his, their*) fault.
5. Neither of the stories was published in (*its, their*) original form.
6. If the drivers do not report the accident, won't (*he, they*) get into trouble?
7. Each girl has to pay for (*her, their*) own lunch.

8. If any senior wants an extra copy, (*he*, *they*) can get one from Mr. Hill.
9. If a driver neglects to report an accident, (*he*, *they*) can get into serious trouble.
10. Neither of them could remember (*his*, *their*) locker number.
11. By the time a boy reaches eighteen, (*he*, *they*, *you*) should be able to think for (*himself*, *themselves*, *yourself*).
12. It is stupid and unfair to judge a person by (*his*, *their*) looks.
13. If anyone dared disobey, (*he*, *they*, *you*) would be fired on the spot.
14. One of the girls had left (*her*, *their*) purse in the library.
15. A person who never expresses (*his*, *their*) opinion probably has none.
16. Each player is responsible for (*his*, *their*) own equipment.
17. If a student doesn't understand, (*he*, *they*, *you*) should ask questions.
18. Did either of your brothers actually promise that (*he*, *they*) would help?
19. Before a person signs (*his*, *their*) name, (*he*, *they*) should read the petition.
20. Every member of the team was asked to tell what (*he*, *they*) thought of the plan.

FILE III: PRACTICE 9. *Be ready to read the following sentences aloud, substituting for each blank the pronoun form —* who *or* whom *— that would be appropriate in formal English.*

1. _____ was elected president of the Boosters?
2. _____ do you suppose was elected president?
3. _____ did the delegates elect as president?
4. Nobody suspected _____ he really was.
5. The man from _____ we bought the pumpkins did not have change.
6. I asked, "_____ is it?" and she answered, "_____ do you think it is?"
7. The reporter to _____ Lewis told his story was skeptical.

8. _____ did the seniors nominate?
9. To _____ should I send my manuscript?
10. He was the teacher for _____ we had the most respect.
11. Farrell hated to deal with people _____ he distrusted.
12. The two students _____ were suspended will be back next week.
13. Maya Angelou, _____ we heard in New York, is the guest of honor.
14. Vote for Dan Hiker, _____ knows the inner-city problems.
15. We voted for Dan Hiker, _____ we felt we could trust.
16. _____ substituted for _____ in the last quarter?
17. With _____ will I be working?
18. _____ was promoted besides Clifford?
19. Officer Spencer, _____ Tracy interviewed next, was more helpful.
20. A Mr. Donald, _____ none of us knew, was to be the new manager.

FILE III: PRACTICE 10. *Be ready to read each of the following sentences aloud, using the pronoun form in parentheses appropriate in formal English.*

1. Otis is the one (*who, whom*) I think is most likely to succeed.
2. Her friends are (*whoever, whomever*) will help her get ahead.
3. Give the package to (*whoever, whomever*) answers the doorbell.
4. Next he hired a young student (*who, whom*) he thought would be reliable.
5. Your next opponent will be (*whoever, whomever*) beats Fischer.
6. Your next opponent will be (*whoever, whomever*) Fischer defeats in this round.
7. The whole town wonders (*who, whom*) is backing Scott.

8. The first five publishers to (*who, whom, which*) he sent his novel returned it.
9. (*Who, Whom*) should I seat next to (*who, whom*)?
10. (*Who, Whom*) do you think you are?
11. Mom had given all her change to the boy (*who, whom*) delivers our groceries.
12. Most of the students to (*who, whom, which*) we sent questionnaires replied.
13. George and Carlos were the only ones (*who, whom*) were hired.
14. (*Who, Whom*) do you suppose would call at this hour?
15. The boys for (*who, whom*) the lecture was meant weren't even there.
16. Nancy Kelly, (*who, whom*) all the critics praised, was truly excellent.
17. Tell (*whoever, whomever*) is collecting that I will pay him on Friday.
18. Mark Ott, to (*who, whom*) he passed the ball, fumbled it.
19. I wondered then (*who, whom*) was lying to (*who, whom*).
20. (*Whoever, Whomever*) he appoints will have full charge.

FILE III: PRACTICE 11.   A RE-DRILL.   *Each of the following sentences has one or more nonstandard pronoun forms. Be ready to read the sentences aloud, substituting standard forms for the nonstandard ones.*

1. Between you and I, her diamonds are fakes.
2. It's always him who gets the blame.
3. In about an hour us girls straightened out the mess.
4. In fact, me and Ron aren't even related.
5. No, I think them on the kitchen table are for you and she.
6. Them are the best cookies she ever made.
7. Him and Jennie told me so theirself.
8. The only ones who spoke up were her and me.
9. Us volunteering to help paint just made Frank and she more suspicious.

10. Neither of the girls wants their picture taken.
11. Say, Ted, them must be the people who own the place.
12. The general hisself gave the order to retreat.
13. Then one of the outlaws he drew a gun.
14. Them are Brussels sprouts, not broccoli.
15. Few teachers are as hard to fool as him.
16. Are them the only shirts you have in stock?
17. Whom would you say is the prettiest of the four?
18. A person should not take credit for work they did not do theirself.
19. If every member sells as many tickets as him, me and her don't have a chance to win.
20. Whenever one of the boys misbehaved, Grandma would make them stand in a corner by theirself.

FILE III: PRACTICE 12. A RE-DRILL. *Be ready to read the following sentences aloud, using the pronoun forms in parentheses appropriate in standard English.*

1. Dad and (*he*, *him*) worked the graveyard shift for years.
2. As usual, Bill ate more pizza than both Jack and (*I*, *me*).
3. Every Saturday (*we*, *us*) boys caddy for Mr. Lenci and (*he*, *him*).
4. The conductor told Sue and (*I*, *me*) he couldn't accept our transfers.
5. Larry did much better on the math problems than (*I*, *me*).
6. Uncle Bill, to (*who*, *whom*) Mom had given the letter, forgot to mail it.
7. Mr. Olstead, with (*who*, *whom*) Dad usually rides to work, is on vacation this week.
8. As you know, either of the men may still change (*his*, *their*) mind.
9. Darrell and (*I*, *me*) made (*ourself*, *ourselves*, *ourselfs*) some hamburgers.
10. The baby usually makes friends with (*whoever*, *whomever*) picks him up.

11. The best mimics in the class were (*he*, *him*) and (*I*, *me*).
12. To this day nobody knows (*who*, *whom*) the informer was.
13. Are (*them*, *those*) the snow tires you were telling about?
14. (*Who*, *Whom*) did you say was sitting behind you and (*he*, *him*)?
15. If a snoop like Harry goes around looking for trouble, (*he*, *they*) shouldn't be surprised when (*he finds*, *they find*) it.
16. Frank doesn't like Pat and (*I*, *me*), but (*we*, *us*) two don't care for Frank either.
17. Wayne offered to drive Marge and (*I*, *me*) home in his new car.
18. Nobody told (*we*, *us*) girls that the picnic had been canceled.
19. Why didn't you and (*he*, *him*) brush (*yourself*, *yourselves*, *yourselfs*) off and keep going?
20. Between you and (*I*, *me*), (*them*, *those*) are the worst tires on the market.

FILE DRAWER 4

modifier usage

a, an

Whether *a* or *an* is right to use with a particular word depends on the beginning sound of that word. If you pronounce to yourself the words *ape, odor, idea, hour,* and *honor,* you will see that each begins with a vowel sound (even though only the first three words begin with a vowel letter). With all words that begin with a *vowel sound, an* is used:

an ape	an idea	an M
an odor	an eagle	an umbrella
an hour	an honor	an FBI man

With words that begin with a *consonant sound, a* is used:

a table	a bottle	a U-boat
a dart	a window	a European
a phone	a hyphen	a one-horse town

Notice that *a* is used with all the words in the last column. Though these words do not begin with a consonant letter, they do begin with a consonant sound.

ADJECTIVE OR ADVERB?

Which of the two boldfaced words at the right should you use in the following sentences?

Mr. King worked _____.	**steady** or **steadily**
Paul takes his job too _____.	**serious** or **seriously**
I checked the meter _____.	**regular** or **regularly**

The boldfaced words in both columns are modifiers. Those in the first column are **adjectives**. Those in the second — with the

-ly ending—are **adverbs**. The way to decide which is the right modifier to use is to figure out what work the modifier does in the sentence. If its work is to modify a noun or a pronoun, the adjective should be used. If its work is to modify a verb, the adverb should be used.

In these sentences the modifiers are being used to tell something about the verb: how Mr. King worked, how Paul takes his job, how often I checked the meter. Therefore the *adverbs* are the modifiers to use:

Mr. King worked **steadily**.

Paul takes his job too **seriously**.

I checked the meter **regularly**.

Compare the italicized modifiers in the following pairs of sentences. Notice that the forms without *-ly* (adjectives) are used to modify nouns and pronouns; the forms with *-ly* (adverbs) are used to modify verbs:

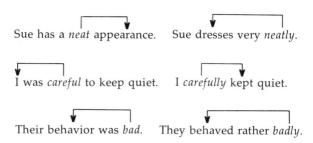

Sue has a *neat* appearance.   Sue dresses very *neatly*.

I was *careful* to keep quiet.   I *carefully* kept quiet.

Their behavior was *bad*.   They behaved rather *badly*.

In nonstandard English the adjective form (without *-ly*) is often used in spots where an adverb form (with *-ly*) is called for:

NONSTANDARD: She talked **sarcastic** to me.
STANDARD: She talked **sarcastically** to me.

Be sure you use the *-ly* form when it is needed.

There are, of course, some adverbs that have two forms—one ending in *-ly* and one that is the same as the adjective. For example:

Walk slowly.   Walk slow.

Jump quickly.   Jump quick.

Aretha sang loudly.   Aretha sang loud.

The two-form adverbs present no problem. Since both forms are standard, either is acceptable. The choice usually depends on which sounds better in a particular sentence. The short form is more likely to be used in commands and conversational sentences. The form with *-ly* is preferred in formal speech and writing.

Remember, too, that the *-ly* ending is not a sure sign that a word is an adverb. Many adjectives also end in *-ly*—for example, *lonely*, *kindly*, *cowardly*, *deadly*, *crumbly*, *manly*.

ADJECTIVE WITH LINKING VERB

Notice the difference in the work done by the italicized verbs in these sentences:

Otis *tasted* the stew.

The stew *tasted* delicious to Otis.

The verb in the first sentence is an **action verb**; it tells what action the subject (Otis) did—he tasted something. But the verb in the second sentence—though it looks the same as the one in the first—is not an action verb; it does not tell what the subject did. The verb in the second sentence is a **linking verb**; its job is to link the descriptive adjective *delicious* to the subject noun *stew*, which it modifies.

113

You have little trouble choosing the correct modifier to tell something about the action verb in sentences like these:

Bruce *looked* **triumphantly** at Joel.

Ann *felt* her way **carefully** down the dark stairs.

He *tasted* the hemlock **reluctantly**.

The detective *smelled* the coffee **suspiciously**.

You use an adverb to describe the action that is done by the subject (to tell *how* Bruce looked at Joel, *how* Ann felt her way, *how* he tasted the hemlock, *how* the detective smelled the coffee).

But sentences like the following—in which the same verbs are used—are sometimes troublesome, even to many users of standard English. Which of the boldfaced modifiers at the right—the adjectives in the first column or the adverbs in the second column—should be used in these sentences?

Bruce *looked* very _____.	**triumphant** or	**triumphantly**
Ann *felt* _____ about the accident.	**bad**	or **badly**
He said the hemlock *tasted* _____.	**bitter**	or **bitterly**
The coffee *smelled* _____.	**peculiar**	or **peculiarly**

The choice depends, of course, on the work the modifier does in the sentence. The verbs in these sentences are not action verbs; their subjects do not do a physical action. Bruce did not look at anything. Ann did not feel (or touch) anything. The hemlock did not taste anything. The coffee did not smell anything. The verbs are linking verbs. The missing modifiers are intended to describe the subjects, not to modify the verbs. Therefore the *adjectives* (the forms without *-ly*) are the modifiers to use:

> Bruce *looked* very **triumphant**.

> Ann *felt* **bad** about the accident.

> He said the hemlock *tasted* **bitter**.

> The coffee *smelled* **peculiar**.

anyplace, everyplace, etc.

The adverbs *anyplace, everyplace, no place,* and *someplace* are labeled colloquial or informal by most usage authorities. In formal English and in careful writing *anywhere, everywhere, nowhere,* and *somewhere* are the forms used.

> COLLOQUIAL: We could sit anyplace we wished.
> WRITTEN: We could sit anywhere we wished.

bad, badly

Bad is the adjective form; *badly* is the adverb form.

It is usual to use an adjective—not an adverb—with a linking verb: "She looked *happy*." "It tasted *delicious*." "I feel *sorry* for him." But in informal speech the adverb *badly* is used after the linking verb *feel* about as often as the adjective *bad*:

> COLLOQUIAL: I feel badly about the misunderstanding.

> COLLOQUIAL: The team felt badly about losing the game.

People seem to feel that the added *-ly* sounds more sincere or elegant.

115

But this usage is not appropriate in formal speech or in writing:

WRITTEN: I feel bad about the misunderstanding.

WRITTEN: The team felt bad about losing the game.

both

In some regional dialects *both* is used in place of *two*:

DIALECT: The both children were injured.
STANDARD: The two (*or* Both) children were injured.

boughten

At one time people grew most of their own food and made most of their own clothes, utensils, soap, cosmetics, medicines, and so on. They seldom bought any of these things in stores. As a result, anything not homemade was special, and words like *boughten* and *store-boughten* were used to call attention to this specialness: "The neighbors were surprised when she served boughten bread." "He was wearing a store-boughten suit."

But today these words are seldom heard except in certain regional dialects, and even there they are disappearing. The reason is obvious: There is nothing special any more about food or clothing or anything else bought at a store. In fact, it is just the reverse. Today we call attention to what is not bought at a store or is not mass-produced. What is special today is to own something "homemade" or "custom-built" or "handcrafted."

COMPARISON OF ADJECTIVES AND ADVERBS

Almost all the adjectives and adverbs in our language have three forms, called the **positive degree**, the **comparative degree**, and the **superlative degree**. The comparative and superlative degrees are formed in two ways: If the modifier is short, the endings *-er* and *-est* are added to the positive (the simple) form:

POSITIVE	COMPARATIVE	SUPERLATIVE
light	lighter	lightest
heavy	heavier	heaviest
soon	sooner	soonest
late	later	latest

If the modifier is long or if it is an adverb ending in *-ly*, *more* and *most* are generally used:

POSITIVE	COMPARATIVE	SUPERLATIVE
beautiful	more beautiful	most beautiful
foolish	more foolish	most foolish
carelessly	more carelessly	most carelessly
gracefully	more gracefully	most gracefully

For a number of modifiers, either way is used. For example:

Adam was *friendly*.

Boris was *friendlier* (or *more friendly*) than Adam.

Carl was the *friendliest* (or *most friendly*) of the three.

Often the emphasis wanted in a particular sentence, as well as the sound, will determine your choice:

My parents were *stricter* than hers.   [Emphasis is on strictness.]

Her father was far *more strict* than Deborah's.   [Emphasis is on degree of strictness.]

But both forms should not be used together. If you use the ending *-er*, do not also use *more*. If you use the ending *-est*, do not also use *most*. Though "double comparison" was usual in Shakespeare's time, it is nonstandard today:

NONSTANDARD: Elmer is more clumsier than Franklin.
STANDARD: Elmer is clumsier than Franklin.
STANDARD: Elmer is more clumsy than Franklin.

Some adjectives and adverbs are compared irregularly. Among the most common are these:

POSITIVE	COMPARATIVE	SUPERLATIVE
bad	worse	worst
badly	worse	worst
far	farther, further	farthest, furthest
good	better	best
many	more	most
much	more	most
well	better	best

The comparative forms are ordinarily used in comparing two persons or things or groups:

Geraldine is *stronger* than Harriet.

Does a battery-driven watch keep time *more accurately* than a spring-driven one?

The Cougars have far *better* hitters than the Cheetahs.

And the superlative forms are ordinarily used in comparing more than two:

Uncle Ira is probably the *most cautious* driver in the country.

Which grow *most rapidly* — oaks, maples, or birches?

Of all the teams in the league, the Jaguars probably get the *least* publicity.

In informal speech the superlative degree is sometimes used in comparing two items:

Naturally Mr. Jack's son was assigned the *largest* of the two offices.

But this usage is not considered appropriate in writing or in formal speech. In written work, use the comparative for two:

Naturally Mr. Jack's son was assigned the *larger* of the two offices.

Note: In formal English, adjectives and adverbs like *perfect, perfectly, unique, round, dead, impossible* are generally used only in their exact, literal meanings — that is, to name qualities that do not vary in degree. A thing is either perfect or not perfect, unique or not unique, dead or not dead. If it is perfect or unique or dead, something else cannot logically be *more* perfect, *more* unique, or *more* dead; it can only be *more nearly* perfect, *more nearly* unique, *more nearly* dead.

But in informal English these words are not always used in their exact, literal sense. *Dead*, for instance, is used to mean not only "without life" but also "dull; quiet." *Unique* is used not only to mean "the only one of its kind" but also "rare; unusual." *Impossible* is used not only to mean "not possible" but also "not easily possible." When the words are used in these broader meanings, they are often compared, as in these sentences:

Keith won the prize for the most unique costume.

I've never been in a deader town.

COMPARISONS: LOGICAL AND ILLOGICAL

1 When making comparisons (showing how or to what degree two or more things are alike or unlike), writers sometimes fail to express their intended meaning accurately. In the following example, the writer obviously intended to compare the prices at two different kinds of stores. But that is not what he has done. Instead he has "illogically" compared prices with a store:

> The prices at a discount store are not always lower than a department store.

To make his comparison "logical," all he needs to do is add two words:

> The prices at a discount store are not always lower than **those at** a department store.

Here is another example of a "false comparison":

> ILLOGICAL: I thought the maid of honor's dress was more attractive than the bride.   [Compares a dress with a person.]
> LOGICAL: I thought the maid of honor's dress was more attractive than the bride**'s**.   [Or: than *that of* the bride; than the bride*'s gown*.]

Though a reader can generally figure out the intended comparison in sentences like these, he may well be annoyed at having to do so. And occasionally he may be unable to do so. To ensure an unannoyed, enlightened readership, always make clear what you are comparing.

2 The following sentence gives an example of another kind of illogical comparison:

> The center practiced harder than anyone on the basketball team.

In this sentence, the center is being compared with "anyone on the basketball team." But "anyone on the team" includes not only the forwards and guards, but the center himself as well. So strictly speaking, or rather, strictly reading, what the sentence says is—

> The center practiced harder than the forwards, the guards, and the center.

Now the writer of the sentence certainly did not mean that the center practiced harder than himself—yet that is what his words say. To make his sentence say what he intended it to say, he should have used the word *else*:

> The center practiced harder *than anyone* **else** on the basketball team.

Whenever you compare persons or things of the same class, make your comparisons logical by using phrases like "than anyone *else*," "than any *other*," "than the *other*."

> ILLOGICAL: Last year more people emigrated from the United Kingdom than from any country in the world. ["Any country" also includes the United Kingdom.]
> LOGICAL: Last year more people emigrated from the United Kingdom *than from any* **other** country in the world.

But phrases with "any" and "other" should not be used after modifiers in the superlative degree:

> ILLOGICAL: Rossiter was the best liked of any other young officer in the battalion. [Or: the best liked of all the other young officers.]
> LOGICAL: Rossiter was the best liked young officer in the battalion. [Or: the best liked of all the young officers; the best liked of the young officers.]

121

Comparisons like these frequently appear in advertising. Watch newspaper and magazine advertisements and listen to radio and TV commercials for a week, and keep track of how many times you hear something like "Klenzo gets clothes cleaner than any washday product on the market" or "The Blankcar men sell more Blankcars than anyone." (A good thing, since it is unlikely anyone else will sell Blankcars.)

But what is acceptable in advertising copy is not necessarily acceptable in other writing. Even though the intended meaning of an illogical comparison is clear enough, it is an unnecessary distraction, annoying to some readers. In proofreading what you write — especially serious writing — it would probably be wise to weed out any illogical comparisons that may have crept in.

complected, complexioned

The word *complected*, used in phrases like "a light-complected girl" and "a dark-complected man," is dialectal. In standard English *complexioned* is used: "a light-complexioned girl," "a dark-complexioned man."

considerable, considerably

Although in speech a clear distinction is not always made between the adverb *considerably* and the adjective *considerable*, in both formal English and informal writing it is:

> The cost of living has risen *considerably* in the last ten years.   [Adverb modifying the verb *has risen*.]

> In the last ten years there has been a *considerable* rise in the cost of living.   [Adjective modifying the noun *rise*.]

In nonstandard English *considerable* is used as an intensifier, but not in standard English:

NONSTANDARD: He was considerable upset.
STANDARD: He was extremely upset.

In informal speech *considerable* is used as a noun:

SPOKEN: We learned considerable from that experience.
WRITTEN: We learned a great deal from that experience.

DOUBLE NEGATIVE

Centuries ago the use of two negative words (*no, not, none, nobody*) to express one negative meaning was standard English. To the best writers — Chaucer and Shakespeare among them — a sentence like this would have seemed quite natural:

She *never* did *nothing* to help us.

But today double negatives are no longer considered acceptable.
The objection to double negatives is not, as generations of schoolchildren were told, that "two negatives make an affirmative." No one (unless he is being stubbornly contrary) would ever take "She never did nothing to help us" to mean "She did a lot to help us." The two negative words make the intended negative meaning only too clear. The real objection to double negatives is that they simply are no longer standard usage. For some time now users of standard English have agreed that one negative word is enough to make a negative statement:

NONSTANDARD: I do**n't** see **nothing** wrong with that plan.
STANDARD: I do**n't** see *anything* wrong with that plan.
STANDARD: I see **nothing** wrong with that plan.

NONSTANDARD: We have**n't** had **no** rain for three weeks.
STANDARD: We have**n't** had *any* rain for three weeks.
STANDARD: We have had **no** rain for three weeks.

123

Most double negatives are easy to spot, since most negative words begin with the letter *n*. But words like *hardly*, *barely*, *scarcely*, and *without*, which do not begin with *n*, are also negative words, and should not be used with other negatives:

> NONSTANDARD: **Hardly nobody** comes to the games these days.
> STANDARD: **Hardly** *anybody* comes to the games these days.

> NONSTANDARD: He found his way back **without no** trouble.
> STANDARD: He found his way back **without** *any* trouble.   [Or: *with* **no** trouble.]

good, well

On bottles of furniture polish, silver polish, copper polish, and shoe polish, you often read this direction:

> Shake *well* before using.

In this sentence the word *well* is used as an adverb telling *how* you should shake the bottle—not *slightly* or *half-heartedly* or *listlessly*, but *well*.

Users of nonstandard English often use the word *good* instead of *well* in such a spot. But users of standard English say:

> Stir it *well*.   [Not: Stir it *good*.]

> It works *well* now.   [Not: It works *good* now.]

> Did you sleep *well*?   [Not: Did you sleep *good*?]

If you are ever tempted to use the word *good* in sentences like these, think of the words "Shake well." They will remind you that when you need a modifier of a verb, you should use the adverb *well*. When you need a modifier of a noun or pronoun, you use the adjective *good*.

It was a *good* game.   Both teams played *well*.

After the linking verb *feel* (I feel _____), a speaker of standard English uses either *good* or *well*, depending on what he means. If he says "I feel *good*," he means that he is in good spirits. There is a bounce to his step, a smile on his face, and a gleam in his eye. But if he says "I feel *well*," he means simply that he is in good health, that he is not sick.

kind, sort

In formal English the singular adjectives *this* and *that* are used to modify the singular *kind* and *sort*:

This kind of car is expensive to operate.

That sort of person makes trouble for everyone.

The plural adjectives *these* and *those* are used only when *kind* and *sort* are plural:

These kinds of errors are inexcusable.

Those sorts of plants are sensitive to cold.

In colloquial usage the plural adjectives are often used with *kind* and *sort*:

Those kind of plants are easier to grow than these kind.

I wouldn't wear those sort of shoes myself.

125

In spite of the fact that this usage is frequently heard in the speech of educated people, it still has only colloquial standing. And though one usage expert says "it is easily forgivable," you would be wise to avoid it in writing, especially formal writing.

kind of [a], sort of [a]

In informal speech *kind of* and *sort of* are often used as adverbs meaning "rather; somewhat; almost; nearly." But this usage is inappropriate in writing:

> SPOKEN: It was kind of cold here yesterday.
> WRITTEN: It was rather cold here yesterday.

> SPOKEN: She seemed sort of annoyed.
> WRITTEN: She seemed somewhat annoyed.

In informal English, especially in speech, *kind of a* and *sort of a* are common:

> What kind of a government do they have?

> I wouldn't be interested in that sort of a trip.

But in formal English the *a* is omitted:

> What kind of government do they have?

> I would not be interested in that sort of trip.

less, fewer

In formal English *less* is used to refer to amount or quantity (to what can be measured) and *fewer* to number (to what can be counted):

We had less time than we thought.
Nora requires much less sleep than the rest of us.

He could have said the same thing in fewer words.
There are fewer accidents now that the street has been widened.

In informal English *less* is rather commonly used instead of *fewer*:

He could have said the same thing in less words.

There are less accidents now that the street has been widened.

Since this use of *less* is frowned on by some people who pride themselves on knowing "good usage," you might want to watch out for it—in your written work anyway.

never

Never means "not ever; at no time." It should not be used when you simply mean *not*:

We got up so late today that we didn't have time to eat breakfast.   [Not: we never had time to eat breakfast.]

nohow

In the sentence "We could nohow interest him in the project," *nohow* is standard. But the word is rarely used in this sense.

Nohow is more often used by speakers of nonstandard English to form double negatives:

NONSTANDARD: He hasn't changed nohow.
STANDARD: He hasn't changed at all.

nowheres, somewheres, etc.

Some speakers of nonstandard English tack an *s* on "where" words: *nowheres, everywheres, anywheres, somewheres*. But the standard forms are *nowhere, everywhere, anywhere, somewhere*.

plenty

Colloquially *plenty* is used as an adverb:

> COLLOQUIAL: We were plenty busy all week.

> COLLOQUIAL: Tanya was plenty surprised.

This adverbial use is avoided in formal English and in most writing:

> WRITTEN: We were extremely busy all week.

> WRITTEN: Tanya was greatly surprised. [Or: very much surprised.]

In writing and in formal speech the noun *plenty* is usually followed by *of* in sentences like these:

> WRITTEN: I thought I had plenty of money when I started out.

> WRITTEN: There was plenty of food left.

In colloquial English the *of* is sometimes omitted:

> COLLOQUIAL: I thought I had plenty money when I started out.

> COLLOQUIAL: There was plenty food left.

pretty

The word *pretty* in the sense of "moderately; fairly; quite; somewhat" is good informal English:

> They gave a pretty good show.

> I felt pretty silly.

But *pretty* in this sense can easily be overused. Watch it, especially in your written work.

them

In nonstandard English *them* is used as a demonstrative adjective, but not in standard English:

> NONSTANDARD: Them boys should mind their own business.
> STANDARD: Those boys should mind their own business.

> NONSTANDARD: Did you make any of them posters?
> STANDARD: Did you make any of those posters?

this here, that there

In standard English *here* and *there* are not used with *this, that, these, those*:

> NONSTANDARD: This here coat is mine. That there one is his.
> STANDARD: This coat is mine. That one [there] is his.

> NONSTANDARD: Are these here tires on sale too?
> STANDARD: Are these tires [here] on sale too?

There is often a temptation to use the word *at* or *to* with the word *where*. The *at* or *to* does add emphasis, as the slangy expression "where it's at" suggests. But since the adverb *where* means "at which place" or "to which place," the *at* or *to* is really unnecessary, and speakers of standard English generally omit it, especially in writing.

Where do they work?   [Not: Where do they work *at*?]

No one knew where he had gone.   [Not: No one knew where he had gone *to*.]

Is that where she is?   [Not: Is that where she's *at*?]

FILE IV: PRACTICE 1.   *Be ready to read each of the following sentences aloud, using the appropriate modifier — adjective or adverb.*

1. Corky can finish the problems (*easy, easily*) in an hour.
2. No wonder your voice sounded (*strange, strangely*)!
3. Doesn't this butter taste a bit (*rancid, rancidly*)?
4. Pete advised the truckers not to act too (*hasty, hastily*).
5. This time Mr. Huntz looked (*suspicious, suspiciously*) at me too.
6. Why does this yarn feel (*different, differently*) from that?
7. The lilacs made the whole house smell (*fragrant, fragrantly*).
8. Oh, he looked (*serious, seriously*) enough, but he talked (*foolish, foolishly*) as usual.
9. How (*delicious, deliciously*) those roasted chestnuts tasted!

10. If he would just talk (*reasonable, reasonably*), we'd listen.
11. How can she look so (*glamorous, glamorously*) after waiting on tables all day?
12. No thanks. Uncle Tito drives so (*reckless, recklessly*) that I'd rather walk.
13. That record doesn't sound so (*bad, badly*) after all.
14. Again he sounded so (*convincing, convincingly*) that she believed him this time too.
15. She moves very (*graceful, gracefully*) for such a heavy woman.
16. Leon could study just as (*easy, easily*) with the TV going as with it off.
17. How (*sarcastic, sarcastically*) he talked to her!
18. She smelled the soup very (*careful, carefully*) and agreed that it smelled (*strange, strangely*).
19. Pronounce each syllable (*clear, clearly*), please.
20. That new perfume of hers certainly smells (*odd, oddly*).

FILE IV: PRACTICE 2. *Be ready to read each of the following sentences aloud, using the appropriate modifier — adjective or adverb.*

1. The chocolate-covered ants didn't taste as (*strangely, strange*) as I thought they would.
2. What smells so (*appetizingly, appetizing*)?
3. That can't be Mike's paper; he doesn't write that (*legibly, legible*).
4. Bloodhounds make good trackers because they can smell so (*keenly, keen*).
5. That little radio of Len's has never worked (*well, good*).
6. The whole family felt (*sadly, sad*) about Oscar's leaving.
7. No wonder this salad tastes (*peculiarly, peculiar*); it has anchovies in it.
8. Why did you leave so (*suddenly, sudden*) last night?
9. He doesn't explain (*clearly, clear*) enough to do us any good.

10. Peggy's voice sounds too (*harshly*, *harsh*) for the part of the little sister.
11. How (*fragrantly*, *fragrant*) those peonies smell!
12. Oh, he likes to wear his glasses; he thinks they make him look (*wisely*, *wise*).
13. Dad expects us to do everything (*perfectly*, *perfect*).
14. The storm had come up so (*suddenly*, *sudden*) that we didn't have time to close the windows.
15. When he's around, Miss Forbes always talks (*sarcastically*, *sarcastic*).
16. What makes this stew taste so (*peculiarly*, *peculiar*)?
17. This time he sounded so (*persuasively*, *persuasive*) that even Frankie believed him.
18. She hasn't been sleeping (*well*, *good*) this past week.
19. Don't feel (*badly*, *bad*) about the accident; it wasn't your fault.
20. In the movie they made from the novel, the story ends (*happily*, *happy*), of course.

FILE IV: PRACTICE 3. *Each of the following sentences has one or two inappropriate modifiers. Be ready to read the sentences aloud, substituting appropriate forms.*

1. Let's sit in the back row so we can get out easy.
2. Carol sounded hysterically, even to herself.
3. But nobody can do everything perfect!
4. When he realized what he had done, Paul felt miserably.
5. What makes Grandpa sound so gruffly?
6. The engine started easy enough, but it didn't run very smooth.
7. Then I realized why they had left so sudden.
8. In fact, a rose by any other name would smell just as sweetly.
9. Try at least to sound convincingly.
10. Now Ron dresses as sloppy as his cousin.
11. Hal felt quite unhappily about the mistake.
12. Did you notice how rude she treated the waitress?

13. They came to the clubhouse rather frequent at first.
14. That dress Marie made fits her pretty good, don't you think?
15. Octopus doesn't taste as peculiarly as I had expected.
16. Larry eats very hearty for someone just recovering from the flu.
17. Why should those berries taste more bitterly than these?
18. I really felt guiltily about breaking the rules.
19. The twins not only look differently, but they talk different.
20. "How stunningly you look in that dress," he said.

FILE IV: PRACTICE 4. *Each of the following sentences has one or two inappropriate modifiers. Be ready to read the sentences aloud, substituting appropriate forms.*

1. She cooks pretty good — for a brand-new bride.
2. Theresa's father works regular now, thank goodness.
3. That snippy teen-ager next door shouldn't talk so disrespectful to her mother.
4. Poor Grandpa doesn't hear too good any more.
5. I just know that clothes won't wear good if they aren't made good.
6. That leftover stew tasted so deliciously that we ate it all up.
7. What makes his voice sound so strangely?
8. Joan can skate almost as good as Peggy Fleming.
9. Don't worry, Mrs. Bruno; my brother can lift that box for you easy.
10. By the end of the summer Perry was speaking Spanish quite fluent.
11. Ever since she got back from that trip, she talks so affected that we can't stand her.
12. For two weeks it rained steady, and then the rain stopped as sudden as it had started.
13. This time he sounded every syllable even more distinct than before.
14. Let's move down; I can't see very good from here.

15. Oh, she feels badly because she didn't do too good in the history test.
16. I wish Blaine could hit as good as he pitches.
17. Old Felix disappeared as sudden as he had appeared.
18. The painter said he could finish the job easy by noon.
19. For years my uncle felt bitterly about the bank failure.
20. His scheme sounds well, I admit, but I'm sure it won't work out good.

FILE IV: PRACTICE 5. *Be ready to read the following sentences aloud, substituting for each blank the appropriate modifier—either* good *or* well.

1. My brother doesn't bowl _____ either, but at least he tries.
2. No one can bowl as _____ as Hugo.
3. Boy, that chili smells _____; I wish I could cook as _____ as you.
4. Look that over _____ before you sign your name.
5. Uncle Hank, who can't hear very _____, really bollixed things up.
6. I'd say he can swim _____ enough to make the team.
7. Everyone in town felt _____ when the Raiders won the championship.
8. He gets along _____ with the other men on the team.
9. I don't think his playing is very _____ for a professional.
10. Can she type _____ enough to suit Mr. Byerly?
11. If only he could sing as _____ as he thinks he does.
12. Uncle Dom does not drive very _____; he is too nervous to be a _____ driver.
13. The colors she chooses look _____ on her, but her clothes seldom fit her _____.
14. The bazaar turned out _____; we all felt _____ about it.
15. My jalopy will run pretty _____ as soon as I fix the valves.

16. Poor Dad hasn't been sleeping _____ the past few nights.
17. Be sure to stir the paint _____, or it will streak.
18. It was a _____ game; everyone played _____.
19. I don't know how _____ his health is, but doesn't he get around amazingly _____ for an eighty-year-old?
20. Say, that tie goes _____ with your new blazer.

FILE IV: PRACTICE 6. *Be ready to read each of the following sentences aloud, using the appropriate comparative form—either adjective or adverb.*

1. After all, my drawing didn't look any (*more peculiar, more peculiarly*) than his.
2. This whipped butter tastes even (*more rancid, more rancidly*) than the regular butter.
3. If only he would talk (*more reasonable, more reasonably*), his employees wouldn't hate him so.
4. I wish Susan would speak (*more distinct, more distinctly*).
5. You'd better attend practice (*more regular, more regularly*), or you'll be kicked off the team.
6. She'd like him to read his part a little (*more natural, more naturally*).
7. Sometimes Mr. Leto behaves (*more childish, more childishly*) than the baby.
8. From now on, Phil will have to take his work (*more serious, more seriously*).
9. Actually, Uncle Dom drives (*more cautious, more cautiously*) than necessary.
10. We tried to figure out why his first speech sounded (*more persuasive, more persuasively*) than his second.
11. We all felt that he treated us (*fairer, more fairly*) than she did.
12. His work always looks (*neater, more neatly*) than Katie's.
13. Al's remarks can't sound any (*more sarcastic, more sarcastically*) than hers.

14. I guess I sounded (*more suspicious, more suspiciously*) than I really was.
15. After that encounter, he looked at us even (*more suspicious, more suspiciously*) than before.
16. His new job looks (*more strenuous, more strenuously*) than his old one.
17. When he is angry, he drives (*more reckless, more recklessly*) than ever.
18. Even my little sister can print (*neater, more neatly*) than that.
19. Well, you could have answered her (*more polite, more politely*) than you did.
20. She'll have to learn to work (*more efficient, more efficiently*) than that.

FILE IV: PRACTICE 7. *Be ready to read the following sentences aloud, using the appropriate modifier.*

1. Our skit was pretty dull, but theirs was even (*worst, worse, worser*) than ours.
2. Neither of the routes is scenic, so we usually take the (*shorter, shortest*) one.
3. Wally likes peaches better than (*any, any other*) fruit.
4. Which one of the men could block their heavy tackle (*easiest, most easy, most easily*)?
5. Buy the other dress—it's the (*smarter, smartest*) of the two.
6. The crook was far more (*handsome, handsomer*) than the detective.
7. Which is (*harder, hardest*) to learn—Russian or Spanish?
8. Which is (*easier, easiest*) to play—a guitar, a mandolin, or a ukulele?
9. The twins are still arguing about which of them is the (*best, better*) chef.
10. It wasn't hard to tell which of the triplets was the (*lazier, laziest*).
11. That morning we got up a little (*more earlier, earlier*) than usual.

12. When Ted and I last measured each other, he was (*tallest*, *taller*).

13. Pork has to be cooked more thoroughly than (*any*, *any other*) meat.

14. Frank finds trigonometry the hardest of (*all his*, *all his other*) courses.

15. I wonder which can run (*fastest*, *faster*) — a camel or an ostrich.

16. The whale is larger than (*any*, *any other*) animal that lives on the earth or in its waters.

17. Ask him which is (*more*, *most*) expensive — the lobster or the steak.

18. He decided that the (*slower*, *slowest*) of the two men was the (*better*, *best*) worker by far.

19. Both of his sisters are pretty, but the blonde is the (*better*, *best*) dancer.

20. They would rather live in Rome than in (*any*, *any other*) city in the whole world.

FILE IV: PRACTICE 8.   *The comparison in each of the following sentences is faulty. Be ready to read the sentences aloud, making whatever changes are necessary to correct the comparisons.*

1. The paint spots on my face were harder to remove than my arms.

2. Most authorities agree that Sarah Bernhardt had more talent than any actress of her era.

3. When Mr. Hansen, the chairman of the board, started working at the company, his salary was smaller than a security guard.

4. The skit presented by the alumni lasted ten minutes longer than the faculty.

5. Mr. Carter, who is an expert welder at Bowen's Shop, earns more money than anyone in the shop.

6. Its tail was quite a bit longer than an antelope.

7. Do I look more better with or without bangs?

8. Well, after the accident Jerry's nose was as large as Cyrano.
9. I'd say a woman's waist is eight to ten inches smaller than a man.
10. *Mannix* is much more exciting than any TV private-eye series.
11. He said the smog in their town is much worse than San Francisco.
12. To tell the truth, my wages were only half as big as Jane.
13. Everyone agreed that Dan's sketches were the best of all the other drawings.
14. This year's fashions are more ridiculous than last year.
15. Rob Mikva, the sports-page editor, worked harder than anyone on the staff.
16. Neil says their boxer is smarter than any dog, no matter what breed.
17. The chili at the Brown Derby is twice as delicious as our cafeteria.
18. In fact, the corridors in the new high school are quite a bit wider than Roosevelt Junior High.
19. We knew that some day she would get even with them, no matter how long it would take; her memory was as long as an elephant.
20. Walt Disney probably won more awards than anyone in the movie industry.

FILE IV: PRACTICE 9. *Be ready to read each of the following sentences aloud, using the form in parentheses appropriate in standard English.*

1. Dad won't let (*any*, *none*) of us use his new camera.
2. Ruth doesn't know (*anything*, *nothing*) about pinochle.
3. But he didn't tell us (*anything*, *nothing*) about a test in spelling!
4. We didn't have (*any*, *no*) snow until the end of December.
5. I (*can*, *can't*) hardly wait for spring vacation.
6. Didn't (*either*, *neither*) of you make the team?

7. Hank hardly (*ever*, *never*) does his own homework.
8. Laura won't (*ever*, *never*) let him copy hers.
9. The print was so small she (*could*, *couldn't*) hardly read it.
10. He didn't have (*any*, *no*) right to talk to us that way.
11. I (*can*, *can't*) hardly believe we won.
12. But you haven't (*ever*, *never*) had the mumps!
13. There (*was*, *wasn't*) scarcely enough room for me, and I'm small.
14. Doesn't Cora work here (*any*, *no*) more?
15. There wasn't (*anybody*, *nobody*) he could turn to for help.
16. If you had been more careful, no one (*would*, *wouldn't*) have been hurt.
17. Frankly, he doesn't have (*any*, *no*) sense.
18. I didn't like (*either*, *neither*) of the twins.
19. Sam won't go (*anywhere*, *nowhere*) without that rabbit's foot.
20. He worked his way through college without (*any*, *no*) help from (*anyone*, *no one*).

FILE IV: PRACTICE 10. *Be ready to read the following sentences aloud, using the forms in parentheses appropriate in standard English.*

1. We were so scared we (*couldn't*, *could*) hardly breathe.
2. Don't you (*never*, *ever*) go bowling (*no*, *any*) more?
3. But hardly (*nobody*, *anybody*) objected at the time.
4. He answered the first ten questions without (*no*, *any*) trouble.
5. At this point the fog was so thick they (*couldn't*, *could*) scarcely see the road.
6. They (*hadn't*, *had*) never dug a well before and (*didn't have*, *had*) no idea of what to do.
7. The next time I looked, he (*wasn't*, *was*) nowhere in sight.
8. No, the Larsons I mean don't live (*nowhere*, *anywhere*) near the bus station.
9. Well, she didn't have (*no*, *any*) right to reverse the charges.

10. (*It isn't, It's*) none of your business, come to think of it.
11. I called twice, but there (*wasn't, was*) no one home.
12. Doesn't that young man have (*no, a*) home of his own?
13. We (*can't, can*) hardly wait for summer vacation to start.
14. I notice that Peggy doesn't (*never, ever*) offer to lend (*none, any*) of us (*none, any*) of her clothes.
15. We left the carnival early because we (*didn't have, had*) no more money.
16. Sam (*wouldn't, would*) never have been hired without your recommendation.
17. Keep on stirring, and the gravy won't have (*no, any*) lumps in it.
18. You won't (*never, ever*) get (*no, a*) bus standing on that corner; this is a skip-stop line.
19. Jerry won't (*never, ever*) say (*nothing, anything*) against Coach Neil.
20. There (*isn't, is*) nobody he admires more than the coach.

FILE IV: PRACTICE 11.   *Be ready to read each of the following sentences aloud, avoiding the double negative it contains.*

1. We looked, but we couldn't find no stores open at that hour.
2. He couldn't have tried no harder than he did.
3. It isn't none of your business, you know.
4. Don't you two kids have no home of your own?
5. My steak was so tough I couldn't hardly cut it.
6. You didn't have no right to tell my dad about it.
7. She thinks she can learn without no effort on her part.
8. There wasn't hardly no one at the pool that day.
9. My guess is they don't know nothing about real estate.
10. How can you plan that kind of trip without no road map?
11. Don't never do such a dangerous thing again.
12. We were broke, so we didn't go nowhere that cost money.
13. If you won't tell nobody, I'll tell you a secret.
14. Don't you and Bill never go swimming no more?

15. The smoke was so thick we couldn't hardly see a thing.
16. I know for a fact he didn't do nothing all day.
17. There wasn't nobody in sight, so I suggested sneaking in.
18. Bonnie likes her hot dog without no mustard.
19. Grandma expected us kids to play Monopoly without no yelling.
20. Didn't neither of you explain what had happened?

FILE IV: PRACTICE 12.   *Be ready to read each of the following sentences aloud, avoiding the double negatives.*

1. I didn't do nothing; he's the one who started it.
2. The twins don't never agree with each other, let alone with nobody else.
3. Don't say nothing about it to no one and you won't get into no trouble.
4. Well, no one is asking for no advice from you neither.
5. The way he diets, your brother won't never lose no weight.
6. I wasn't thinking of nobody in particular.
7. Somehow they managed to get along without no help from nobody.
8. We must have a poor connection; I can't hardly hear a word you're saying.
9. Why didn't no one never complain before?
10. Sam couldn't find neither of the maps.
11. She told me that she wouldn't answer none of their questions.
12. You didn't see no alligators, did you?
13. Mitch always had plenty of money, but he wouldn't never lend us none.
14. As far as I know, they didn't have no friends, and they didn't want none neither.
15. We couldn't hardly believe our eyes!
16. No, our town isn't nowhere near Bloomington.
17. In fact, that poor fellow couldn't have worked no faster than he did.

18. All I can say is that we never had no trouble understanding Pedro.
19. No, thank you, I don't care for no mustard neither; I don't never use it.
20. We found our way there without no trouble.

FILE IV: PRACTICE 13.   *Be ready to read each of the following sentences aloud, choosing from the forms in parentheses the one that would be appropriate in standard written English.*

1. Dad was (*plenty, very*) crabby again last night.
2. Where were you (*going, going to*) in such a hurry?
3. I'm afraid the (*both, two*) programs are on at the same hour.
4. How did you like (*that there, that*) hairdo of hers?
5. Antoinette reported seeing a suspicious-looking, (*dark-complexioned, dark-complected*) man in the back entryway when she came in.
6. There was (*plenty, plenty of*) excitement at the track meet yesterday.
7. (*Them, Those*) sweaters you like are on sale at Carson's this week.
8. Casey seemed (*rather, kind of*) embarrassed about winning.
9. I've looked (*everywheres, everywhere*), and I haven't found (*them, those*) negatives yet.
10. Just because I have (*less, fewer*) classes this semester, don't think that I have (*less, fewer*) homework.
11. Why are (*them there, them, those*) chairs more expensive than the others?
12. I despise (*those, that*) kind of people, don't you?
13. In Paris the faucet marked with (*a, an*) C is the hot water, and the one marked with (*a, an*) F is the cold.
14. We got to Field's just fifteen minutes before it closed, so we (*never had, didn't have*) time to look at the porch furniture.
15. Don't ask us about Len; we never know where (*he's at, he is*).
16. The (*less, fewer*) shirts there were to be ironed, the better she liked it.

142

17. I know he was (*considerable, extremely*) annoyed when he saw what (*them, those*) rabbits had done to his garden.
18. Well, if (*them, those*) coins aren't in the desk, they must be (*someplace, somewhere*) else, so keep looking.
19. There are (*less, fewer*) complaints now that Mr. Kane is in charge.
20. I (*never saw, didn't see*) (*those, them*) footprints when I came in.

FILE IV: PRACTICE 14.   *Be ready to read each of the following sentences aloud, using the appropriate form.*

1. We're getting (*no place, nowheres, nowhere*) fast.
2. Yes, you can go to that restaurant — if you have (*plenty, plenty of*) money.
3. I can't stand (*those, that*) sort of people.
4. We looked (*everywheres, everywhere*) for the car keys, without any luck.
5. (*Them, Those*) jeans you like are on sale at Wieboldt's.
6. There were (*fewer, less*) complaints than last year.
7. I didn't like him (*nohow, at all*), and I let him know it.
8. Can't you see (*that there, that*) flaw at the top?
9. He was so changed that I (*never recognized, didn't recognize*) him until he spoke.
10. Do the batteries come with (*them, those*) robots?
11. Aunt Blanche was (*considerable, quite*) upset about Pat's lying to her.
12. He's not the (*kind of a, kind of*) supervisor I would like.
13. The coach thinks the (*both, two*) fellows were equally to blame.
14. Why should they feel (*bad, badly*); it wasn't their fault.
15. Well, the jigsaw puzzle you worked had (*less, fewer*) pieces.
16. We stayed home; there was (*nowheres, nowhere*) to go in Roseburg.
17. The play turned out much (*more better, better*) than we had dared hope.

18. It was the (*worse, worst*) movie we had ever seen.
19. I was so sleepy during that first-period class that I (*never heard, didn't hear*) one word of his lecture.
20. Oh, is that where (*he's at, he is*) this year?

FILE IV: PRACTICE 15. A RE-DRILL. *Each of the following sentences has one or more nonstandard forms. Be ready to read the sentences aloud, substituting standard forms for the nonstandard ones.*

1. When Pete said that his hamburger didn't taste well, the waiter looked indignantly.
2. Where are they staying at in Las Vegas?
3. I had less spelling errors than anyone in our room.
4. J. Ralph Letty is one of the ten most wealthiest men in the world.
5. We were so sleepy by that time we couldn't hardly keep our eyes open.
6. There must be a more simpler way to wash a dog!
7. Where are you going to after the show?
8. That isn't hardly the kind of a play that I enjoy.
9. How can anyone eat them tomatoes without no salt?
10. Jim doesn't have no beard neither, but he insists on shaving every day anyways.
11. Which is more smarter — a dolphin or a chimpanzee?
12. Why did them women look at me so peculiar?
13. That there dent on his fender was so small you couldn't hardly see it.
14. Our apartment is more smaller than theirs and has less windows.
15. I'll bet them alligator shoes cost plenty money.
16. If that cough gets any worser, you'd better take some of this here medicine.
17. The train got in so late this evening that Dad never had time to buy a paper.
18. Them there flowers he brought certainly smell oddly.

19. Actually Ruth doesn't know nothing about football or hockey.
20. I can't hardly believe that cold water freezes more slower than hot water.

FILE IV: PRACTICE 16. A RE-DRILL. *Be ready to read each of the following sentences aloud, using the form in parentheses appropriate in standard English.*

1. One thing is sure: he always pays his bills (*prompt*, *promptly*).
2. Joan swims rather (*good*, *well*) for a beginner.
3. The doctors had to work (*swift*, *swiftly*).
4. The coach looked at me so (*sad*, *sadly*) that I really felt (*guilty*, *guiltily*) about breaking training.
5. You didn't see (*any*, *no*) poison ivy (*anywhere*, *nowhere*), did you?
6. The next time, get someone who knows the alphabet (*good*, *well*) enough to file everything (*efficient*, *efficiently*).
7. Well, he (*can*, *can't*) hardly expect her to look (*beautiful*, *beautifully*) when she's washing walls!
8. Cal's trouble is that he can't see (*good*, *well*) enough to tell whether the hedge is trimmed (*even*, *evenly*) or not.
9. Which is (*more*, *most*) dangerous — a crocodile or an alligator?
10. I hate to admit it, but his excuse sounded (*more plausible*, *more plausibly*) than mine.
11. Uncle Alvin, who couldn't hear very (*good*, *well*), made the situation (*worse*, *worser*, *more worse*) by asking me to repeat the remark.
12. With only four minutes between classes today, we (*never had*, *didn't have*) time to hang around our lockers and talk.
13. Sam has (*plenty*, *plenty of*) work of his own to do.
14. Pete won't trust (*anybody*, *nobody*) (*any*, *no*) more.
15. Mr. Barnes usually orders a lettuce-tomato sandwich without (*any*, *no*) mayonnaise.

FILE DRAWER 5

dictional demons

accept, except

Because these words are similar in sound, people sometimes confuse them. *Accept* is always a verb. It means "take or receive; consent to receive; agree to; say yes to":

> The captain of the team, Gloria Goff, accepted the trophy.

> Did the girls accept your apology?

> He predicts that China will accept the terms of the treaty.

> She has decided to accept the invitation to address Congress.

Except is most commonly used as a preposition meaning "but":

> The store is open every day except Saturday.

Except is also used in formal English as a verb meaning "exclude; leave out; excuse":

> No one will be excepted from the test.

affect, effect

This is another word pair whose similarity in sound and spelling causes confusion. *Affect* is always a verb; it is most frequently used to mean either "act on; influence" or "pretend to have or feel":

> When Grandfather doesn't feel like answering the children's questions, he affects deafness.

Effect is used chiefly as a noun, meaning "result; consequence; power to produce results; influence":

Does criticism from viewers have any effect on TV programing?

In formal English *effect* is also used as a verb, meaning "bring about or make happen":

The Surgeon General's report effected a change in many people's attitude toward smoking.

all the farther, all the faster, etc.

Such phrases are localisms — expressions used mainly in one section of the country. People in other sections use instead *as far as*, *as fast as*, etc.

LOCALISM: Hawk Lake is all the farther we will go.
STANDARD: Hawk Lake is as far as we will go.

LOCALISM: Is that all the louder you can play?
STANDARD: Is that as loud as you can play?

allude, refer

Both *allude* and *refer* mean "to mention something in a way that directs attention to it." But *allude* means "to call attention *indirectly*"; *refer* means "to call attention *directly*":

Though she did not refer to either of them by name, everyone in the audience knew which men she was alluding to when she spoke of "two highly placed officials who have repeatedly tried to manipulate the news."

American

When we talk about a citizen or a product of some country — of Australia, for example, or of Spain — we generally use a convenient term derived from the name of the country: "an Australian," "a Spaniard," "a Spanish shawl." But no similarly convenient term can be formed from the name of our country, the United States. So the term *American*, from the name of the continent, is used. This term is inaccurate, as citizens of other North American countries and of Central and South America are quick to point out. After all, they are just as "American" as the citizens of the United States. Even so, the term is so convenient and has been in use for so long that it will certainly continue to be used. But when strict accuracy is called for or when the term might be considered offensive, you may want to substitute other words — for example, "a U.S. citizen," "a product of the United States," and not "an American," "an American product."

being as, being that

Speakers of some dialects use the phrases *being as* and *being that* in sentences like these:

> DIALECT: Being as Sheila really needed a job, I was glad she was the one hired.

> DIALECT: Being that Charlie gets airsick, he does not enjoy flying.

In standard English, *since* or *because* or *as* would be used:

> STANDARD: Since Sheila really needed a job, I was glad she was the one hired.

> STANDARD: Because Charlie gets airsick, he does not enjoy flying.

between, among

Among is used in referring to three or more people, places, or things:

> The remaining food was divided equally among the six survivors.

Between is generally used to refer to only two items or two groups of items:

> She was forced to choose between her two closest friends.

> Officer Olivera managed to arrange a truce between the two gangs.

When it is used to refer to more than two, the word *between* suggests that the people, places, or things are to be considered two at a time:

> After months of discussion between the three nations, a trade agreement was drawn up.

Between is followed either by a plural (*between the rows, between halves*) or by two expressions joined by *and*—not by *or* or *to*:

> ILLOGICAL: He had to choose between losing fifteen pounds or losing his place on the first string.
> LOGICAL: He had to choose between losing fifteen pounds and losing his place on the first string.

> ILLOGICAL: The average heart pumps between four to five quarts of blood a minute.
> LOGICAL: The average heart pumps between four and five quarts of blood a minute.

Although we commonly hear such expressions as "between each cabin" and "between every act," it would be more logical to say:

There is a narrow walk between each cabin and the next.

The clowns entertain after every act. [Or: between acts.]

by (at, to)

In nonstandard English, especially in speech, *by* is sometimes used in a spot where *at* or *to* is used in standard English:

NONSTANDARD: We usually eat Thanksgiving dinner by Aunt Kay's house.
STANDARD: We usually eat Thanksgiving dinner at Aunt Kay's house.

NONSTANDARD: You have to go by a post office to register a letter.
STANDARD: You have to go to a post office to register a letter.

censor, censure

These words are sometimes confused. When you mean "to examine a letter, book, movie, TV program, etc., and remove or prohibit anything objectionable in it" or when you are referring to a person with the power to make such an examination and prohibition, the word to use is *censor*:

During wartime the mail of military personnel is censored to make sure that useful information cannot fall into enemy hands.

The network censor ruled that the violent scenes had to be cut from the program before it could be shown.

When you mean "to express strong disapproval; to condemn" or when you are referring to "an expression of strong disapproval or criticism," the word to use is *censure*:

The legislature officially censured their colleague for accepting money and favors from a lobbyist.

He was untroubled by the censure of people whose views he did not respect.

A person can be censured but not censored.

center around (or about)

Center around and *center about* are informal idioms:

Most of the stories center around (*or* about) his prowess as a fighter.

In formal English *center on* or *center in* is used:

Most of the stories center on his prowess as a fighter.

All family authority was centered in the mother.

credible, credulous

The endings of these words can help you keep them distinct. Remembering that *-ible* means "able to be; capable of being" can help remind you that *credible* is the one that means "able to be believed; believable":

It was a credible story, even if it wasn't true.

Keeping in mind that *-ous* means "full of; given to" can help you remember that *credulous* means "given to believing; too ready to believe":

> He shouldn't tell those wild stories to someone as credulous as Sue; she won't realize he is joking.

discover, invent

Although at one time *invent* could be used in the sense of "discover," these verbs now have distinct meanings. To *discover* is to "see, find out, or learn of for the first time something already in existence":

> The story that Wilhelm Roentgen discovered X rays by accident is untrue.

To *invent* is to "think up, make, or work out something that did not exist before":

> A Swiss chemist, Jacques Brandenberger, invented cellophane around 1900.

disinterested, uninterested

Though in colloquial usage you will sometimes hear the word *disinterested* used as a synonym for *uninterested*, careful speakers and writers make a distinction between these words. *Disinterested* is used to mean "having no selfish interest or personal feelings in a matter and therefore no reason or desire to be anything but strictly impartial":

> It is hard to believe that a legislator who owns stock in several insurance companies can be disinterested when it comes to a bill to curb insurance-company profits.

155

Since Mr. Skelly has nothing to gain or lose from the sale, he should give you a disinterested opinion of the car's value.

Uninterested is used to mean "not interested":

How can anyone who is uninterested in a job do well at it?

He was completely uninterested in my opinion, and told me so.

A good rule of thumb is that if you can substitute the word *impartial, disinterested* is the word you need.

economic, economical

These modifiers have different meanings. *Economic* is generally used to mean "having to do with business or economics — the production, distribution, and consumption of wealth":

Opponents of the President claimed that his economic policies had brought on the recession.

Economical is used to mean "avoiding waste of money, time, etc.; thrifty":

How can she claim that eating dinner at a restaurant every night is more economical than eating at home?

eminent, imminent

About once a week you will hear a newscaster or a news commentator say *imminent* when he means *eminent*. He knows what meaning he intends, but he gets the words confused, probably because of the similarity in their pronunciations. The word *eminent* /em'ə nənt/ means "distinguished; outstanding":

> Before taking up his new duties, the ambassador sought the advice of two eminent authorities on Middle East affairs.

Imminent /im'ə nənt/ means "likely to happen without delay; threatening to occur soon":

> However, an hour after the engineers announced that there was no imminent danger of a flood, the dam burst.

When you have trouble with a pair of words like these, try using a memory device—perhaps two phrases like "*emi*nent *em*peror" and "*imm*inent *im*prisonment"—to help keep them straight.

flaunt, flout

Flaunt means "to show off; parade; display ostentatiously":

> The industrialists flaunted their wealth by showering their wives with furs and jewels and building ugly, ornate mansions.

Do not use *flaunt* when you mean *flout*—"to treat with contempt; scornfully disregard":

> When the arrogant young lawyer flouted the judge's ruling, he was cited for contempt of court.

formally, formerly

Strangely enough, people who never confuse the words *formal* and *former* sometimes get the *-ly* forms *formally* and *formerly* confused. *Formally* indicates the manner in which something is done—"in a formal way":

> Everyone knew how the vote had turned out, but the results had not been formally announced yet.

Formerly indicates time; it means "in the past; some time ago":

> The present dean was formerly a teacher of chemistry at Knickerbocker Community College.

good and

Colloquially, *good and* is used as an intensifier meaning "very; extremely; entirely; thoroughly":

> COLLOQUIAL: We were good and hungry by then.

> COLLOQUIAL: Be sure you get the windows good and clean.

But this usage is not appropriate in most writing other than dialogue:

> WRITTEN: We were very hungry by then.

> WRITTEN: Be sure you get the windows thoroughly clean.

half

The standard idioms are *a half* and *half a(n)*:

> In a half hour we had made only a half dollar.

> In half an hour we had made only half a dollar.

In speech the article *a* is frequently used both before and after *half*, as in *a half a ton, a half a dollar*. But such repetition is unnecessary and should generally be avoided in writing.

healthful, healthy

Strictly speaking, these words have distinct meanings. *Healthful* means "giving health" or "good for the health," and *healthy* means "having or showing good health":

> The article said that walking is one of the most healthful forms of exercise.

> I don't know how he stays healthy; his diet is anything but healthful.

Often, however, the word *healthy* is used in the sense of "healthful":

> Who would argue that smoking is healthy?

The use of *healthy* in the sense of "large; considerable" (a healthy income, a healthy respect) is considered colloquial.

hopefully

The adverb *hopefully* originally meant only "in a hopeful manner":

> We waved hopefully at car after car, but not one stopped.

> Hearing the Good Humor bell, he looked hopefully at his father.

But recently it has come to be used also in the sense of "it is hoped":

> Hopefully, Mr. Macklin will resign.

> Hopefully, the whole thing will blow over.

However, since some people disapprove of this usage, you would be wise to avoid it if you think there is a chance it will annoy your audience and distract them from the point you are making.

illusion, allusion, delusion

Because of the similarity in pronunciation of *illusion* and *allusion*, people sometimes confuse these words. But they are quite different in meaning. An *illusion* is a "false impression" or "deceptive appearance":

> Her conversation, her clothes, and her behavior created an illusion of wealth.

> That the sun rises in the east and sets in the west is an illusion, of course.

An *allusion* is an "indirect reference to someone or something generally familiar":

> The poem is filled with allusions to mythology and the Bible.

Sometimes *illusion* is confused with *delusion*, which is a "false belief or opinion":

> One of the characters in *Arsenic and Old Lace* has the delusion that he is Teddy Roosevelt.

imply, infer

Careful speakers and writers distinguish between these two words, using *imply* to mean "indicate without saying outright," and *infer* to mean "draw a conclusion by reasoning":

> Madeline's warm smile implied that she was pleased to see us.

> We inferred from Senator Coker's speech that he favored busing.

However, *infer* has been used so often in the sense of "imply" that many dictionaries record "imply" as a secondary meaning of *infer*.

notorious, famous

Both these words refer to someone or something widely known—but for different reasons. *Notorious* generally means "widely known in an unfavorable way":

> I knew little about her family except that her great-grandfather had been a notorious cattle rustler.

Famous means "widely known for accomplishment or excellence":

> She had one ambition—to become a famous racing driver like Stirling Moss.

Famous should not be used in referring to someone obviously well known to almost everyone:

> As [the famous] P. T. Barnum is supposed to have said, "There's a sucker born every minute."

But in writing about someone whose fame was limited to a certain period of time or to a certain field that readers might not be familiar with, *famous* would be appropriate to use:

> Uncle Burt said the entertainers reminded him of Smith and Dale, a famous comedy team of vaudeville days.

to home, at home

Saying that a person is *to home* (meaning that he is "in his house") is a nonstandard usage. Say either that he is *at home* or simply that he is *home*:

> NONSTANDARD: We are always to home on Sunday night.
> STANDARD: We are always at home (*or* home) on Sunday night.

FILE V: PRACTICE 1. *Decide which of the words in parentheses at the end of each sentence is the right one to use in the sentence. Be ready to read the sentences aloud, substituting for the blanks the words that you decide on.*

1. I am sure there is no one _____ upstairs. (*at home, to home*)
2. His great-grandfather used to be the sheriff in this county in the days of the _____ Ma Barker gang. (*famous, notorious*)
3. A mirage is an optical _____ caused by atmospheric conditions. (*allusion, illusion*)

4. He labors under the _____ that he is the boss in his house. (*allusion, delusion*)

5. They will arrive, _____, by six at the latest. (*hopefully, I hope*)

6. Was Marvin _____ last night? (*to home, home*)

7. _____ the directors and their wives always dressed _____ for the stockholders' banquet. (*formally, formerly*)

8. How would you divide five dollars _____ seven boys? (*among, between*)

9. Spinach may be _____, but I'm sure I can be _____ without it. (*healthful, healthy*)

10. I can wash, wrap, and pack _____ dozen glasses in _____ hour. (*a half a, half a, a half*)

11. Our state's most _____ swindler, Terrence Crombley, once lived in that hotel. (*famous, notorious*)

12. Vertical stripes help to create an _____ of slenderness. (*allusion, illusion*)

13. The furniture in the attic was divided _____ Aunt Harriet, Aunt Sue, and Mother. (*among, between*)

14. The city of Peking was _____ called Peiping. (*formally, formerly*)

15. You'd better not exaggerate around Tim; he's not the _____ freshman his twin brother is. (*credible, credulous*)

16. Well, _____ we arrived quite late, we had to sit in the balcony. (*being as, since*)

17. His tone _____ that he did not believe a word she said. (*inferred, implied*)

18. She _____ from the look on his face that he did not believe a word. (*inferred, implied*)

19. Gerry was _____ secretary to the district attorney. (*formally, formerly*)

20. In 1898 Marie and Pierre Curie _____ radium. (*discovered, invented*)

FILE V: PRACTICE 2. *Decide which of the words in parentheses at the end of each sentence is the right one to use in the sen-*

tence. Be ready to read the sentences aloud, substituting for the blanks the words that you decide on.

1. Gloria said she was pleased, but her manner _____ she was not. (*implied, inferred*)
2. All members of the debate team are _____ from the weekly class debates. (*accepted, excepted*)
3. Anyone who believed such a story must have been _____ indeed. (*credible, credulous*)
4. When he was only twenty-two, McCormick _____ a reaper that proved highly successful. (*discovered, invented*)
5. Both sides agreed to leave the decision to _____ arbiter. (*a disinterested, an uninterested*)
6. You have to go _____ the dean's office to sign up for that trip. (*by, to, at*)
7. The British accent she _____ is intended to create an _____ of a high-society background. (*affects, effects*) (*allusion, illusion*)
8. Every Saturday night we go _____ my aunt's house for supper. (*by, to, at*)
9. "Your letters will be _____ as a matter of course," said the lieutenant. (*censored, censured*)
10. Don's father didn't _____ to Coach Brennan by name, but he was certainly _____ to him in his crack about a "moonlighting gym teacher." (*allude, refer*) (*alluding, referring*)
11. I wish someone would explain to me the difference _____ *continual, continuous,* and *continued* — if there is a difference. (*among, between*)
12. This week the committee is going to meet _____ our house. (*by, to, at*)
13. Our congressman should be _____ for making such irresponsible, inflammatory speeches. (*censored, censured*)
14. Between November of 1970 _____ June of 1972 the train fares were increased twice. (*and, to*)
15. Dr. Garren advised him to move to a more _____ climate. (*healthful, healthy*)

16. At this turn of events, the prime minister became _____. (*good and mad, extremely angry*)
17. The new nation was as much in danger of _____ collapse as of invasion. (*economic, economical*)
18. A showdown was _____, and there was little chance that the prime minister would remain in the good graces of the king. (*eminent, imminent*)
19. According to Jerry, a bad law should be_____. (*flaunted, flouted*)
20. Everyone _____ Sally thinks the school should _____ honor-roll students from attendance at assembly programs. (*accept, except*)

FILE V: PRACTICE 3. *Decide which of the words in parentheses at the end of each sentence is the right one to use in the sentence. Be ready to read the sentences aloud, substituting for the blanks the words that you decide on.*

1. Raw carrots may be _____, but my family won't eat them. (*healthful, healthy*)
2. Waukegan is _____ this train goes. (*all the farther, as far as*)
3. Air pollution _____ everyone's health to some extent. (*affects, effects*)
4. What _____ does all this adverse criticism have on TV programing? (*affect, effect*)
5. The Elmhurst Pattersons were enormously wealthy but lived very modestly; their New York cousins _____ their wealth. (*flaunted, flouted*)
6. The laboratory is under the direction of Dr. Morgan Furthwold, the _____ bacteriologist, best known for his discovery of virus QD-2. (*eminent, imminent*)
7. We will raise at least five thousand dollars, _____. (*hopefully, we hope*)
8. Alice went through the cookbook, looking for recipes for _____ meals. (*economic, economical*)

9. Are you planning on staying _____ this evening? (*to home, home*)

10. The story _____ the theft of a painting from the Louvre. (*centers around, centers on*)

11. When the estate is divided _____ his many relatives, no one will get much. (*among, between*)

12. Joe always had to pay the full fare, _____ he was so tall for his age. (*being that, since*)

13. At first Philip was _____ in their ideas; but after attending a meeting or two, he became enthusiastic. (*disinterested, uninterested*)

14. The President's _____ advisers thought that raising taxes would check inflation. (*economic, economical*)

15. Realizing that an invasion was _____, Ganz took immediate steps to get his family out of the country. (*eminent, imminent*)

16. Discuss it with her; if she is _____ in running for office herself, she may want to campaign for Mrs. Urbanek. (*disinterested, uninterested*)

17. The news story _____ that Kirby was not scrupulously honest. (*inferred, implied*)

18. If you divide the work _____ the members of the club, it will get done in time. (*among, between*)

19. I _____ from her comments that she disapproved of Mr. Hanley. (*implied, inferred*)

20. If the men work _____ every day, they can finish the job by Saturday noon. (*good and hard, very hard*)

FILE V: PRACTICE 4. *Decide which of the words in parentheses at the end of each sentence is the right one to use in the sentence. Be ready to read the sentences aloud, substituting for the blanks the words that you decide on.*

1. By the end of the trip even the passengers who were bundled up in furs were _____. (*good and chilled, thoroughly chilled*)

2. Why don't you ask your doctor to suggest a _____ diet for you? *(healthful, healthy)*

3. This is a gossipy biography, filled with fascinating anecdotes about his circle of friends — a miscellaneous assortment of _____ writers, _____ swindlers, celebrated musicians, _____ scientists. *(famous, notorious)* *(famous, notorious)* *(eminent, imminent)*

4. Most of the waitresses there were making between fifty _____ seventy dollars a week. *(and, to)*

5. Keep in mind that the dispute _____ their unwillingness to cooperate. *(centers around, centers on)*

6. I couldn't figure out who Mr. Pierce was _____ to when he spoke so sarcastically of "our neighborhood pharisees." *(alluding, referring)*

7. We'll be rehearsing tonight _____ Mitch's house. *(by, to, at)*

8. When her boyfriend is around, Bonnie always _____ a great interest in sports. *(affects, effects)*

9. Dave had to choose between mowing the lawn _____ washing the car. *(and, or)*

10. One of her jobs as faculty adviser was to _____ the copy for the gossip column. *(censor, censure)*

11. Well, _____ Sharon is a spoiled brat, she always expects to have her own way. *(being that, since)*

12. Did the increase in price have any _____ on the sales? *(affect, effect)*

13. No one is to be _____ from doing the lab work. *(accepted, excepted)*

14. Ten dollars is _____ he is willing to pay for the bike. *(all the more, as much as)*

15. The _____ visit of an _____ patron of the arts had the whole staff of the academy in a dither. *(eminent, imminent)*

16. First came disputes with personnel; then came _____ problems. *(economic, economical)*

17. How could you be so _____ as to believe such a fantastic, _____ story! *(credible, credulous)* *(incredible, incredulous)*

18. It was hard to tell which the prince enjoyed more — _____ his wealth or _____ the advice of his councilors. (*flaunting, flouting*)

19. The new members will be _____ initiated tomorrow. (*formally, formerly*)

20. I wonder if our state legislature will dare to _____ the members involved in this real-estate deal. (*censor, censure*)

FILE V: PRACTICE 5. ON YOUR OWN. *The terms enclosed in parentheses are words (or phrases) that are commonly confused, in great part because of the similarity in sound or spelling. Read each sentence and decide, from the context, which term is the right one to use in the sentence. You will have to refer to a dictionary for help with any of the terms you are unfamiliar with or unsure of.*

Be ready to read the sentences aloud, substituting for the blanks the words that you decide on — pronounced correctly.

1. "That young man will just have to learn _____ his temper," muttered Mr. Peske, "or he'll be fired before the end of the week." (*to curb, to curve*)

2. As soon as the chairman managed to restore some order in the room, we _____ with the discussion. (*preceded, proceeded*)

3. The crane operator, who looked about eighteen years old, managed his machine _____. (*with incredible skill, with incredulous skill*)

4. Most of the students at Milburn Academy came from enormously wealthy families and _____ such things as skiing vacations, trips to Europe, cabins in the mountains, and cottages on the lake. (*took for granite, took for granted*)

5. J. D. Wilkins, the owner of the company, was a mean, bad-tempered fellow who wanted to be the _____ figure at every meeting. (*dominant, dominate*)

6. When questioned by a reporter, the author insisted the characters in his novel were _____ and any resemblance to real people was purely coincidental. (*facetious, fictitious*)

7. To Uncle Joseph, a wedding anniversary is a time for
_____, and he had brought a bottle of champagne so we
could drink a toast to the Salvatis. (*sediment, sentiment*)

8. The villagers again warned Van Boek of the difficulties and
of the dangers of this part of the climb, but he decided to go
on _____. (*irregardless, regardless*)

9. The _____ assigned to the case was a young unknown
from the district attorney's office. (*persecutor, prosecutor*)

10. The movie was _____ from a short story he had written
when he was a student at Bread Loaf. (*adapted, adopted*)

11. The more you help him, the more he will expect you to do;
it's a _____. (*vicious circle, vicious cycle*)

12. Why are they complaining? They've lived here enough
years to know that in this area ninety-degree temperatures
are _____ in July. (*seasonal, seasonable*)

13. The biscuits, served with honey from their own _____,
were a pleasing testimony of the fact that the way to a man's
heart is through his stomach. (*apiary, aviary*)

14. The following day the _____ department warned all the
employees that there was some danger of the plant's being
sold. (*personal, personnel*)

15. Marvin Kohler was elected president of the club by _____
vote. (*an anonymous, a unanimous*)

16. Of course, if your savings account is very small, a difference
of a quarter of 1 percent in interest payments is _____.
(*negligent, negligible*)

17. The second act ends with Thomas More's farewell to his
family—a _____ scene. (*heart-rending, heart-rendering*)

18. He explained that since there was no _____ for giving
school credits for doing part-time clerical work, he'd have
to consult the school board. (*precedence, precedent*)

19. No, the manager did not say in so many words that the
strikers would be fired, but the threat was _____ in what
he did say. (*explicit, implicit*)

20. Terry's report and Mr. Procter's observations did not
_____ in all respects, and we don't know which is the
more accurate account. (*jibe, jive*)

FILE DRAWER 6

mechanics

CAPITALIZATION CHECKLIST

Animals

> USE CAPITALS: **Smokey Bear, Champion Land Loyalty** of **Bellhaven, Mickey Mouse, Crackers**
> DON'T USE CAPITALS: a famous **bear**, a champion **collie**, a **mouse**, our **parrot**

Brand Names

> USE CAPITALS: a **Chevrolet Camaro, Jell-O, Pepsi-Cola**
> DON'T USE CAPITALS: a Chevrolet **sedan**, a **gelatin dessert**, two glasses of **cola**

Buildings

> USE CAPITALS: the **Hunt Hotel**, atop the **Prudential Building**, the **National Gallery** of **Art**, at **McCormick Place**
> DON'T USE CAPITALS: a downtown **hotel**, atop a tall **building**, an **art museum**, at an **exhibition center**

Business Firms

> USE CAPITALS: **Sears, Roebuck** and **Co.**; **Merrill Lynch, Pierce, Fenner** & **Smith, Inc.**
> DON'T USE CAPITALS: a **general merchandising firm**, a **brokerage house**

Churches and Churchgoers

> USE CAPITALS: **Temple Emanu-El, St. John** the **Divine**, the **Jama Masjid, Presbyterians, Roman Catholics**, and **Mennonites**
> DON'T USE CAPITALS: a **synagogue**, an Episcopalian **cathedral**, a **mosque, church members**

Compass Terms

USE CAPITALS: a specialty of the **South**, moved to the **North**, thinks like an **Easterner**, the climate in the **Midwest**
DON'T USE CAPITALS: drove **south** two blocks, a **northern** breeze, the **east** window, turned **west** at the stoplight

Correspondence

USE CAPITALS: **Dear Madam:**   **Sincerely** yours, **Yours** very truly,
DON'T USE CAPITALS: My **dear** Miss Wiggins: Yours **sincerely,**   Very **truly yours,**

Days, Months, etc.

USE CAPITALS: a **Friday** in **June**, next **December**, the **Fourth** of **July, Christmas Eve, Rosh Hashanah**
DON'T USE CAPITALS: a day in **summer**, next **winter**, the **first** of the **month**, on the **eve** of graduation, a religious **holiday**

Government Bodies and Agencies

USE CAPITALS: the **Central Intelligence Agency**, the **Department** of **State**, the **United States Senate**, the **Atomic Energy Commission**
DON'T USE CAPITALS: a **government agency**, a Cabinet **department**, a **legislative body**, an **independent commission**

Historical Events, Periods, Documents

USE CAPITALS: **World War II**, the **Renaissance**, the **Magna Charta**
DON'T USE CAPITALS: a **war**, a **historical period**, a **charter**

Institutions

> USE CAPITALS: **Northwestern University**, at **Cook County Hospital**, the **Ford Foundation**, the **New York Public Library**
> DON'T USE CAPITALS: an urban **university**, at a **county hospital**, a private **foundation**, the largest **public library** in the country

Languages, Nationalities, and Tribes

> USE CAPITALS: **Urdu**, **Brazilian**, **Sioux** and **Iroquois**
> DON'T USE CAPITALS: a foreign **language**, his **nationality**, two Indian **tribes**

People

> USE CAPITALS: **Sally**; **Jonathan K. Werner**; **Robin Hood**; **Clarence Day, Jr.**
> DON'T USE CAPITALS: a young **girl**, his best **friend**, a legendary **outlaw**, the **author**

Personal Titles

> USE CAPITALS: showed it to **Father**, for her **Aunt Agatha**, while visiting **Grandma**
> DON'T USE CAPITALS: showed it to her **father**, for his **aunt** and **uncle**, while visiting our **grandma**

> USE CAPITALS: to **Mayor Walsh** of **Arbor**; Good morning, **Mayor**; invited **Director Burke**; from **Superintendent Lopez**; the **President** of the **United States**; **Prime Minister Manley** of **Jamaica**
> DON'T USE CAPITALS: greeted the **mayor** of the **village**, a **director** named Burke, from the **school superintendent**, the **president** of the **bank**, will elect a new **prime minister**

Places

USE CAPITALS: visit **Yellowstone National Park**; down the **Amazon River**; climb **Mount Everest**; **Paris, Illinois**; **Lake Champlain**; the **Northwest Territory**; on **Fifth Avenue**; the **United States** of **America**

DON'T USE CAPITALS: visit the first **national park**, down a jungle **river**, climb a **mountain**, a small **town**, a **lake**, a **five-state region**, on our **street**, our **country**

Political Terms

USE CAPITALS: **Whig**, the **Democratic** platform, a **Republican** convention, a **Socialist**

DON'T USE CAPITALS: a former **political party**, the **democratic** method, a **republican** form of **government**, a **socialist** proposal

Proper Adjectives

USE CAPITALS: **Euclidean** geometry, a **Benedictine** abbey, **Mephistophelian** intrigue

DON'T USE CAPITALS: **plane** geometry, a **cloistered** abbey, **devilish** intrigue

Quotations

USE CAPITALS: Then he asked, "**Who** is next?"

DON'T USE CAPITALS: "Who," he asked, "**is** next?"

Religious Terms

USE CAPITALS: **Christianity** and **Taoism**; the **Book** of **Mormon**; the **Book** of **Job**; the **Old Testament**; thanked **Our Lord, God**

DON'T USE CAPITALS: **religions**; a **sacred book**; a **book** of the Bible; a **division** of the Bible; for Ra, one of the **gods**

176

School Terms

USE CAPITALS: beat **Taft High School**, enjoyed **History 211** and **Music 101**, took **Russian** and **French**, failed **American Writers II**, for the **Astronomy Club**, going to the **Senior Picnic**

DON'T USE CAPITALS: beat a rival **high school**, enjoyed **history** and **music**, took **algebra** and **botany**, studied American **writers**, a **club** for **astronomy** buffs, a **picnic** for **seniors**

Ships, Trains, and Planes

USE CAPITALS: **R.M.S. Queen Elizabeth 2**, the **Empire Builder**, **Vostok VI**, the **Spirit** of **St. Louis**

DON'T USE CAPITALS: an **ocean liner**, a **passenger train**, a Russian **spacecraft**, a famous **airplane**

Titles of Publications, etc.

USE CAPITALS: "**Fools Rush In**," "**And Life Goes On**," **World Without End**

DON'T USE CAPITALS: "Down **in the** Valley," "Jack **and** Jill," Golfing **with the** Pros

PLURALS OF NOUNS

1 Regular patterns. Most noun plurals are written in one of two ways:

a) If the sound /s/ or /z/ is added to the singular in saying the plural form, the letter *s* is added in writing it:

graph — graphs	racer — racers
picnic — picnics	pearl — pearls
Democrat — Democrats	handstand — handstands
Mr. Smith — the Smiths	Mrs. Lang — the Langs

b) If the sound /iz/ is added—as it is to singulars ending in the sound /ch/ (*patch*), /sh/ (*marsh*), /s/ (*alias*), /ks/ (*box*), or /z/ (*buzz*)—the letters *es* are added in writing the plural:

batch—batches	compass—compasses
wish—wishes	fox—foxes
atlas—atlases	topaz—topazes
chintz—chintzes	Mr. Waters—the Waterses

c) If the singular form ends in the letter *e*, an *s* is always added in writing the plural, no matter what sound is added in speech:

snake—snakes   battle—battles   nose—noses

2 Irregular patterns. There are a few groups of nouns that do not follow the regular patterns:

a) Though the plural forms of words ending in the letter *y* are all pronounced the same way—with a /z/ sound at the end—the plurals are not all written in the same way. When a noun ends in *y* preceded by a vowel, *s* is added:

joy—joys	display—displays
attorney—attorneys	guy—guys

When a noun ends in *y* preceded by a consonant, the written plural is formed by changing the *y* to *i* and adding *es*:

lady—ladies	hobby—hobbies
spy—spies	penny—pennies
battery—batteries	treaty—treaties

Names of people are exceptions to this rule:

Don't you know the *McGarrys*?   [Not: *McGarries*.]

There were five *Nancys* on the list.   [Not: *Nancies*.]

b) The spelling of the plural forms of nouns ending in *o* varies. Most often the plural is written in the regular way—by adding *s*:

stereo—stereos   avocado—avocados
portfolio—portfolios   poncho—ponchos
shampoo—shampoos   silo—silos

But a few are formed by adding *es*:

potato—potatoes   echo—echoes
tomato—tomatoes   torpedo—torpedoes
hero—heroes   Negro—Negroes

And still others are written either way—with an *s* or an *es*:

banjo—banjos or banjoes   cargo—cargoes or cargos
tornado—tornadoes or tornados

c) The plural forms of nouns ending in *f* and *fe* also vary. Some are written with *s*, others with *ves*, and a few with either *s* or *ves*:

WITH *s*:   chief—chiefs   safe—safes
giraffe—giraffes   sheriff—sheriffs

WITH *ves*:   thief—thieves   half—halves
life—lives   shelf—shelves   wolf—wolves

WITH *s* OR *ves*:   scarf—scarfs or scarves
wharf—wharves or wharfs   hoof—hoofs or hooves

d) The plurals of a small group of nouns are formed by a change in spelling. For example:

woman—women   child—children
fireman—firemen   mouse—mice

foot — feet   goose — geese
eyetooth — eyeteeth   musk ox — musk oxen

e) A few nouns have the same form in the singular and the plural. For example:

a Swiss — several Swiss
one old moose — three young moose
this bellows — a dozen bellows

f) The plurals of most compounds — words like *half brother*, *half-truth*, and *halfback* — are formed by adding *s* at the end:

half brothers   half-truths   halfbacks
close-up — close-ups   six-year-old — six-year-olds
great-aunt — great-aunts   two-by-four — two-by-fours
first mate — first mates   night school — night schools

But there are some exceptions. When a compound consists of a noun followed by a modifier (either a word or a phrase), the noun is usually made plural, since it is the most important word:

attorney general — attorneys general
court-martial — courts-martial
bill of sale — bills of sale
mother-in-law — mothers-in-law
hanger-on — hangers-on
justice of the peace — justices of the peace

The exceptions are becoming fewer, however. According to one well-known linguist, there is a trend toward forming the plural of all compound words by adding *s* at the end. So you will occasionally see compounds like *attorney general*, *court-martial*, and *mother-in-law* written with a regular plural ending (*attorney generals*, *court-martials*, *mother-in-laws*). But this has not yet become the general practice with all such compounds.

g) Some nouns borrowed from foreign languages have English plural endings, others foreign endings, and still others have both:

ENGLISH PLURALS: asylum — asylums virus — viruses
encyclopedia — encyclopedias casino — casinos
prima donna — prima donnas

FOREIGN PLURALS: datum — data basis — bases
alumnus — alumni chassis — chassis
monsieur — messieurs

BOTH: stadium — stadiums or stadia
index — indexes or indices Nisei — Niseis or Nisei
virtuoso — virtuosos or virtuosi

In scientific and formal writing, the foreign plurals of words that have both forms are more likely to be used. But in other situations the English plurals are more common and are the appropriate forms to use.

h) Either *s* or *'s* is added to numbers, signs, letters, and words discussed as words. The *'s* is preferred after all small letters and those capital letters that would be confusing if *s* alone were added:

three 4s or three 4's	the 1970s or the 1970's
some +s or some +'s	two \$s or two \$'s
learning the ABCs	learning the three R's
I's that look like *L*'s	four *i*'s in *Mississippi*
two *u*'s in *vacuum*	too many *and*'s and *so*'s

Note: The important thing to keep in mind is that the plurals of some nouns are irregular. If you are uncertain how to write a particular plural, turn to a dictionary. Most dictionaries show irregular forms (either right after the entry word or at the end of the entry) and indicate whether there is more than one accepted form.

POSSESSIVE FORMS

1 The possessive of a singular noun or indefinite pronoun is generally formed by adding an apostrophe and an *s* after it:

one lady	one lady's wristwatch
the cat	the cat's whiskers
a day	a day's pay
the halfback	the halfback's injury
her son-in-law	her son-in-law's appetite
the Surgeon General	the Surgeon General's report
Mr. Ness	Mr. Ness's plan
anybody	anybody's guess

With singular proper names ending in *s*, usage is divided. Sometimes only an apostrophe is added: Mr. Ness' plan. But most often both an apostrophe and an *s* are used except with the names of Jesus and Moses and Greek names of more than one syllable ending in *es*:   Jesus' words, Achilles' heel.

2 The possessive of plural nouns ending in *s* is formed by adding an apostrophe:

the ladies	the ladies' handbags
the nurses	the nurses' caps
twenty cents	twenty cents' worth
the Nesses	the Nesses' lawn
the Rotzolls	the Rotzolls' trailer
the donkeys	the donkeys' brays

If the plural does not end in *s*, both an apostrophe and an *s* are used:

the firemen	the firemen's axes
her sons-in-law	her sons-in-law's jobs
the children	the children's protests
three mice	three mice's tails
the geese	the geese's honks

182

3 To show joint ownership by two or more, the last noun is made possessive:

> Dr. Hamby and Dr. Blain's waiting room   [They share it.]
> Tom, Dick, and Harry's boat   [The three men own it together.]
> the machinists and aerospace workers' union   [The two groups form one union.]

But to show separate ownership, each noun is made possessive:

> Dr. Hamby's and Dr. Blain's offices   [Each one has an office.]
> Tom's, Dick's, and Harry's cars   [Each owns his own car.]
> the plumbers' and electricians' unions   [Each group has its own union.]

4 The personal pronouns and the relative and interrogative pronoun *who* have special possessive forms, spelled without the apostrophe:

> USED BEFORE NOUNS: my, your, his, her, its, our, their; whose

> USED ALONE: mine, yours, his, hers, its, ours, theirs; whose

5 The possessive may also be formed by using a phrase with *of*:

> the leaves of the plant (the plant's leaves)
> the laughter of the children (the children's laughter)

The *of*-possessive is more common with names of inanimate objects than the *'s*-form, but both are used. The *'s*-form is more common with names of people, although both are used. For example:

the ring of the telephone   the telephone's ring
Shakespeare's plays   the plays of Shakespeare

In general, choose the form that sounds best in the sentence.

6 The 's-form and the *of*-form are often combined, especially with *that* or *this*:

that old jacket of Ned's   those stupid jokes of Al's
this great plan of Mary's   a friend of my sister's

PRONUNCIATION

Which of the two pronunciations given after each of the words in the following list do you use? (The pronunciation key on page 188 will help you interpret the dictionary respellings.)

either   /ē′ŦHər/ *or* /ī′ŦHər/
creek   /krēk/ *or* /krik/
juvenile   /jü′və nəl/ *or* /jü′və nīl/

Is the other pronunciation—the one you do not use— "wrong"? No. It is just as "right" as yours. A number of English words—*either, creek,* and *juvenile* among them—have more than one standard pronunciation. You probably use the pronunciation that is common in your section of the country. If you were to move to another area, you might find that the other pronunciation is the more usual one there.

Here are some more examples of words with "variant" pronunciations. Which pronunciation do you use for each? Have you ever heard the other?

abdomen   /ab′də mən/ *or* /ab dō′mən/
adult   /ə dult′/ *or* /ad′ult/

advertisement   /ad'vər tīz'mənt/ *or* /ad vėr'tis mənt/
ally (n.)   /al'ī/ *or* /ə lī'/
almond   /ä'mənd/ *or* /am'ənd/ *or* /äl'mənd/ *or* /al'mənd/
buoy   /boi/ *or* /bü'ē/
Caribbean   /kar'ə bē'ən/ *or* /kə rib'ē ən/
exquisite   /ek'skwi zit/ *or* /ek skwiz'it/
gratis   /grat'is/ *or* /grā'tis/
greasy   /grē'sē/ *or* /grē'zē/
lever   /lev'ər/ *or* /lē'vər/
maraschino   /mar'ə skē'nō/ *or* /mar'ə shē'nō/
naphtha   /nap'thə/ *or* /naf'thə/
pajamas   /pə jä'məz/ *or* /pə jam'əz/
permit (n.)   /pėr'mit/ *or* /pər mit'/
qualm   /kwäm/ *or* /kwälm/
route   /rüt/ *or* /rout/
sputnik   /sput'nik/ *or* /spút'nik/
tomato   /tə mā'tō/ *or* /tə mä'tō/
via   /vī'ə/ *or* /vē'ə/

Some words with variant pronunciations are words taken into English from foreign languages. Generally, if the foreign pronunciation of such a word presents no problems, it is kept. But often a foreign pronunciation proves difficult. Then the word is given a second pronunciation, an Anglicized one. Here are a few examples:

aficionado   Spanish /ä fē'thyō nä'dō/
             English /ə fē'syə nä'dō/

antipasto   Italian /än'tē päs'tō/
            English /an'tē pas'tō/

au jus   French /ō zhʏ'/
         English /ō zhü'/ *or* /ō jüs'/

bologna   Italian /bō lōn'yä/
          English /bə lō'nē/ *or* /bə lō'nə/

185

bratwurst   German /brät′vůrsht′/
            English /brat′wərst/ or /brät′wərst/

dauphin   French /dō faɴ′/
          English /dô′fən/

Gestapo   German /gə shtä′pō/
          English /gə stä′pō/

gourmand   French /gür mäɴ′/
           English /gůr′mənd/

maestro   Italian /mä es′trō/
          English /mī′strō/

maharanee   Hindi /mə hä′rä′nē/
            English /mä′hə rä′nē/

mantilla   Spanish /män tē′ə/
           English /man til′ə/

messieurs   French /mā syœ′/
            English /mes′ərz/

Mexico   Spanish /mä′hē kô′/
         English /mek′sə kō/

modus operandi   Latin /mō′důs ō′pe rän′dē/
                 English /mō′dəs op′ə ran′dī/

Paris   French /pa rē′/
        English /par′is/

picador   Spanish /pē′kä thôr′/
          English /pik′ə dôr/

première   French /prə myar′/
           English /pri mir′/

Quebec French /kā bek'/
        English /kwi bek'/

sauerbraten German /zou'ər brät'n/
             English /sour'brät'n/ *or* /sou'ər brät'n/

sayonara Japanese /sä'yô nä'rä/
          English /sī'ə när'ə/

smorgasbord Swedish /smœr'gōs bürd'/
             English /smôr'gəs bôrd'/

strudel German /shtrü'dl/
         English /strü'dl/

vodka Russian /vôd'kä/
       English /vod'kə/

Yom Kippur Hebrew /yōm' kē pür'/
            English /yom kip'ər/

Most school and college dictionaries today list the standard variant pronunciations of a word. So you can easily check any pronunciation you are in doubt about. If a pronunciation is not listed, it is probably not standard. Take, for example, a frequently heard pronunciation of the word *athlete* — /ath'ə lēt/. You will not find this pronunciation given as a variant. It is nonstandard. The standard pronunciation is /ath'lēt/ — with two syllables, not three.

The following list shows the standard and nonstandard pronunciations of some words that are frequently mispronounced. Look through the list to spot any nonstandard pronunciations you may be using unawares.

	STANDARD	NONSTANDARD
across	/ə krôs'/	/ə krôst'/
admirable	/ad'mər ə bəl/	/ad mī'rə bəl/

Africa	/af'rə kə/	/af'ėr kə/
arthritis	/är thrī'tis/	/är thėr ī'tis/
architect	/är'kə tekt/	/är'chə tekt/
ask	/ask/	/aks/
athletics	/ath let'iks/	/ath ə let'iks/
candidate	/kan'də dāt/ *or* /kan'də dit/	/kan'ə dāt/
champion	/cham'pē ən/	/cham pēn'/
chance	/chans/	/chanst/
chimney	/chim'nē/	/chim'ə nē/
comparable	/kom'pər ə bəl/	/kəm par'ə bəl/
disastrous	/də zas'trəs/	/də zas'tėr əs/
drowned	/dround/	/droun'did/
elm	/elm/	/el'um/
film	/film/	/fil'um/
genuine	/jen'yü ən/	/jen'yü wīn/
height	/hīt/	/hīth/
hindrance	/hin'drəns/	/hin'dėr əns/
incongruous	/in kong'grü əs/	/in'kon grü'əs/
indicative	/in dik'ə tiv/	/in'di kā'tiv/
indict	/in dīt'/	/in dikt'/
irreparable	/i rep'ər ə bəl/	/ir'rə par'ə bəl/
library	/lī'brer'ē/	/lī'ber'ē/
license	/lī'sns/	/lī'sn/
mischievous	/mis'chə vəs/	/mis chē'vē əs/
modern	/mod'ərn/	/mod'rən/

---

hat, āge, fär; let, ēqual, tėrm; it, īce; hot, ōpen, ôrder; oil, out; cup, pùt, rüle; ch, child; ng, long; sh, she; th, thin; ᴛʜ, then; zh, measure; ə represents *a* in about, *e* in taken, *i* in pencil, *o* in lemon, *u* in circus; ʏ as in French *du* (pronounce ē with the lips rounded as for English ü in rule); œ as in French *peu* (pronounce ā with the lips rounded as for ō); ɴ as in French *bon* (the ɴ is not pronounced, but shows that the vowel before it is nasal); ʜ as in German *ach* (pronounce k without closing the breath passage).

nuclear	/nü'klē ər/ or	/nü'kyü lər/
	/nyü'klē ər/	
once	/wuns/	/wunst/
perspiration	/pėr'spə rā'shən/	/pres'pə rā'shən/
preferable	/pref'ər ə bəl/	/pri fėr'ə bəl/
prescription	/pri skrip'shən/	/pėr skrip'shən/
probably	/prob'ə blē/	/prob'ə lē/
quantity	/kwon'tə tē/	/kwä'nə tē/
radiator	/rā'dē ā'tər/	/rad'ē ā'tər/
represent	/rep'ri zent'/	/rep'er zent'/
southern	/su͜ŦH'ərn/	/su͜ŦH'rən/
strength	/strength/	/strenth/
superfluous	/su̇ pėr'flü əs/	/su̇'pər flü'əs/
theater	/thē'ə tər/	/thē ā'tər/
usually	/yü'zhü ə lē/	/yü'zhü lē/
western	/wes'tərn/	/wes'trən/

PUNCTUATION CHECKLIST

USE PERIODS—

1) with abbreviations:

Mr. and Mrs. Roger Perez, Jr.   Eloise P. Norton, M.D.

Dr. Norton   St. Anthony   1001 B.C.

2) after a statement, a command, a request, or an indirect question:

Babe Ruth started his career as a pitcher.

Sit down and be quiet.

Will you please send an answer by return mail.

He asked me how long I planned to stay.

USE A QUESTION MARK —
after a direct question:

> How long do you plan to stay?

> Babe Ruth started out as a pitcher, didn't he?

> Marvin made the dinner?

USE AN EXCLAMATION MARK —
to give emphasis to a word, phrase, or sentence:

> Wow!　　Good grief!　　Look out!

> What a beautiful day!　　He can't be serious!

USE COMMAS —
 1) to separate items in a series:

> Every Tom, Dick, and Harry has heard the story by now.

> She picked up each melon, smelled it, shook it, and then put it back on the table.

> We had no idea who he was, where he had come from, or what he wanted.

[*Note:*　Commas are not needed when all the items are joined by coordinating conjunctions:　The sound grew louder *and* louder *and* louder.　Did he mean you *or* me *or* himself?]
 2) before the coordinating conjunction that joins the main clauses in a compound sentence:

> Harry leaned back, and the chair tipped over.

> President Grant was honest, but many of his appointees were not.

It couldn't have cost more than five dollars, or Velma wouldn't have bought it.

[*Note:* If the clauses are short and there is no possibility of misunderstanding, a comma is not needed: He washed and I dried.]

3) to set off parenthetical expressions:

Clifford, don't forget, was still locked in the closet.

Sylvia was no fool, after all.

However, the evidence was mostly circumstantial.

4) to set off a noun of address:

Do you agree, Dr. Watson?

Sorry, my boy, but you are dead wrong.

Ladies and gentlemen, please be seated.

5) to set off an appositive:

Zelda also did a commercial for Zilch, a soft drink.

The river, just a trickle in late fall and winter, becomes a raging torrent in late spring and summer.

6) to set off the second and all following items in a date or an address:

On July 27, 1958, he went out to buy a newspaper and was never seen again.

The signed affidavits should be sent to Baker and Son, 71 Doyle Lane, Hilo, Hawaii 96720, by May 10.

7) after an introductory adverb clause:

> Although he didn't need the money, Salwich took the job.

> Before she left, she told her neighbors what she thought of them.

8) after an introductory verbal phrase:

> To buy more wire and metal for his experiments, Marconi sold his shoes.

> Before taking the stand, the witness conferred with her lawyer.

> Hoping to get even, we challenged them to another game.

9) to set off a nonrestrictive adjective clause:

> Milo, who has no sense of humor, looked at me very disapprovingly.

> Panama became an independent country in 1903, when it revolted from Colombia.

[*Note:* *Restrictive* adjective clauses are not set off: Someone *who has no sense of humor* can be pretty hard to live with at times.]

10) to set off a nonrestrictive participial phrase:

> Sylvester, standing in the shadow of the big elm, saw the whole thing.

[*Note:* *Restrictive* participial phrases are not set off: Anyone *standing in the shadow of the big elm* would not be seen.]

11) after the closing in a letter:

Sincerely yours,   Cordially,   With love,

12) after the salutation in a personal letter:

Dear Carl,   Dear Mrs. Foley,   Sweetheart,

13) to set off a speaker's directly quoted words from the rest of the sentence:

Then he said, "I'm innocent."

"I'm innocent," he insisted.

"I can see," he said sadly, "that you don't believe me."

14) for clearness:

Just the day before, Carlos had turned in his resignation.   [To prevent: Just the day before Carlos had turned in. . . .]

Where she was, was no concern of mine.   [To prevent the reader from tripping over the repeated word.]

USE A SEMICOLON—
1) between two parts of a compound sentence if they are not joined by a coordinating conjunction:

The Hindu troops could not eat beef; the Muslim troops could not eat pork.

Think first; then speak.

Theoretically the Czar had absolute power; actually, however, he was dependent on the nobility.

2) between two parts of a compound sentence joined by a coordinating conjunction if either clause is long and complicated:

> McGuffy, discouraged by his lack of success in the ring, wanted to quit fighting; but his manager, Sam Rolo, who was deeply in debt, begged him to fight just once more.

3) to separate items in a series if the items contain commas:

> Henry's first three wives were Catherine of Aragon, whom he divorced; Anne Boleyn, whom he had beheaded; and Jane Seymour, who died in childbirth.

> They hope to establish offices in Springfield, Massachusetts; Springfield, Ohio; Springfield, Illinois; and Springfield, Missouri.

USE A COLON —
1) after the salutation in a business letter:

> Dear Sir: Dear Mrs. Pluckley: Gentlemen:

2) to introduce a formal quotation:

> Perhaps Thomas Carlyle put it best when he wrote: "Originality is a thing we constantly clamour for, and constantly quarrel with."

3) to introduce a list of appositives that comes at the end of a sentence:

> In his report the building inspector cited three main housing-code violations: cracked and falling plaster, broken plumbing fixtures, and bare electrical wiring.

> Two topics Mrs. Vandiver absolutely refused to discuss: politics and religion.

[*Note:* The colon is used before a list *only* when the items are appositives. When they are complements or objects, no punctuation mark is used before them: The two topics Mrs. Vandiver absolutely refused to discuss were politics and religion.]

USE DASHES —

1) to indicate an abrupt change in thought:

> The first step is — no, come to think of it, that's not the first step.

> I had originally planned — but that's too long a story.

2) to set off parenthetical expressions that make abrupt interruptions:

> The horse — Harvey isn't much of a rider — kept going in circles.

> About once a month — sometimes oftener — there is a bombing scare.

> Erma Brightside — didn't you once share a locker with her? — won the latest state lottery.

> The following year Tony sold the store — what a mistake that proved! — and bought a run-down fruit ranch.

3) to call attention to or emphasize an appositive or nonrestrictive modifier:

> Grandfather earned twelve dollars a week — a very good salary in those days.

> That evening — after Dad had mowed the lawn and carried out the garbage cans — Morrie's limp miraculously disappeared.

4) to set off an appositive or nonrestrictive modifer that has commas in it:

> When the prairie dogs hear their sentries' danger call—
> *skip*, *skip*, *skip*—they dive into their burrows.

> All day long the flicker parents forage for tidbits—grubs, larvae, and juicy berries—to feed their always famished fledglings.

> The collision—which I heard, but did not see—involved six cars.

USE PARENTHESES—
1) to enclose numbers or letters that mark items in a series:

> The treaty between Spain and the United States had three main provisions: (1) Cuba was to be independent, (2) Puerto Rico and Guam were to be ceded to the U.S., and (3) the Philippine Islands were to be sold to the U.S. for twenty million dollars.

> If the source is a book, the footnote should include (a) the author's name, (b) the title of the book, and (c) the page or pages referred to.

2) to enclose a tucked-in explanation or side remark:

> Sharecroppers gave a part of their crops (generally one fourth to one third) as rent.

> The falling boulders pushed two buses (both empty, fortunately) off the road and down the embankment.

> Mrs. Greatleach (have you ever heard a more appropriate name?) sponged on the Westmoreland family for a good six months.

1) to enclose the exact words of a speaker:

> "Are you quitting already?" he asked.

> Suddenly the foreman yelled, "Run!"

> "The dinner," she said, "was overpriced and undercooked."

[*Note:* Quotation marks are not used in an indirect quotation: She said that the dinner was overpriced and undercooked.]

2) for titles of stories, articles, chapters, short poems, songs:

> "Papa and the Bomb"   "The Magic in Your Name"

> "In Time of Crisis"   "From This Day On"

USE SINGLE QUOTATION MARKS —
for a quotation that comes inside another quotation:

> "Who said, 'Fifty million Frenchmen can't be wrong'?"

> "No," Tom said, "I think 'Ask the man who owns one' was the slogan of an automobile company."

> "You could have at least yelled 'Look out!'" I said.

USE UNDERLINING —
1) for titles of books, magazines, newspapers, pamphlets, movies, radio and TV programs, plays, and long poems:

> <u>Great Expectations</u>   <u>Life</u>   <u>The Cherry Orchard</u>

2) for words (or letters or numbers) used as words:

> There is no <u>z</u> in <u>surprise</u>.

SPELLING

1 Many people grumble about the irregularities of English spelling. To hear them tell it, unless a writer has a photographic memory, he has to guess whether or not he should put two *m*'s in *swimming*, for example, or an *e* in *ninety*. There are no "rules," say the grumblers, to help the writer out. Though there are irregularities in English spelling, it is inaccurate to say that there are no "rules" to use as guides. Let's look at a few that apply to large groups of commonly used words. Becoming familiar with them can help a writer avoid many common spelling errors.

a) *Doubling final consonants.* When a word of one syllable ends in a single consonant preceded by a single vowel, the consonant is doubled before a suffix beginning with a vowel:

win + er = winner	swim + ing = swimming
sad + est = saddest	drop + ed = dropped
big + ish = biggish	rob + ery = robbery

If the word has more than one syllable, the final consonant is doubled only if the accent is on the last syllable:

be gin' + er = beginner	oc cur' + ence = occurrence
o mit' + ed = omitted	con trol' + ing = controlling
de ter' + ent = deterrent	re gret' + able = regrettable

Words like *e quip'* and *a quit'* come under this rule because the *u*, which has a /w/ sound, is considered a consonant. If a suffix beginning with a vowel is added to one of these words, the final consonant is doubled:

equipping	equipped	equipper
aquitting	aquittal	aquittance

Words like *depend* and *respect* (which end in two consonants), *appear* and *succeed* (which have two vowels preceding

198

the final consonant), and *develop* and *credit* (which are not ac-
cented on the last syllable) do not double the final consonant:

dependence	appearance	developer
respected	succeeding	creditable

b) *Final silent* e.   When a word ends in a final unpro-
nounced *e*, the *e* is dropped before a suffix beginning with a
vowel:

forge + er = forger	virtue + ous = virtuous
stripe + ed = striped	scarce + ity = scarcity
excuse + able = excusable	insure + ance = insurance
come + ing = coming	educate + or = educator
large + ish = largish	store + age = storage
refuse + al = refusal	adhere + ence = adherence

There are a few exceptions: the *e* is kept in words like *dyeing*
and *singeing* (to keep them distinct from *dying* and *singing*) and
in words like *noticeable* and *advantageous* (to keep the /s/ sound
of the *c* and the /j/ sound of the *g*).

Before a suffix beginning with a consonant, the final silent *e* is usually kept:

hope + ful = hopeful	nice + ly = nicely
care + less = careless	retire + ment = retirement
aware + ness = awareness	nine + ty = ninety

A few commonly used words are exceptions: *ninth*, *truly*, *duly*,
argument, *wholly*.

c) *Words with* y.   When a word ends in *y* preceded by a
consonant, the *y* is changed to *i* before a suffix beginning with
a consonant:

steady + ly = steadily	merry + ment = merriment
happy + ness = happiness	penny + less = penniless
bounty + ful = bountiful	glory + fy = glorify

The same change is made before the suffixes *-es, -ed, -er,* and *-est*:

worry + es = worries   pretty + er = prettier
study + ed = studied   silly + est = silliest

But before the suffix *-ing*, the *y* is kept:

hurrying   spying   modifying

d) *Adding prefixes.* The prefixes *dis-, mis-,* and *un-* end with a single consonant. When one of these prefixes is attached to a base word beginning with the same consonant, there will be two *s*'s or two *n*'s:

dis + satisfy = dissatisfy   dis + solve = dissolve
mis + spell = misspell   mis + state = misstate
un + natural = unnatural   un + named = unnamed

If the base word begins with some other letter, there will be only one *s* or one *n*:

disabled   mismatch   untrue

e) *Adding suffixes.* No letter is dropped from a base word ending in a consonant when the suffix *-ness* or *-ly* is added:

stern + ness = sternness   usual + ly = usually
mean + ness = meanness   cool + ly = coolly
open + ness = openness   normal + ly = normally

But remember that if the base word ends in *y* preceded by a consonant, the *y* is changed to *i*: *unruliness, flimsily.*

f) Ei *and* ie. Use *ie* when the sound is long *e* (as in *bee*):

believe   niece   shriek   siege
chief   thief   piece   grievance

A few common exceptions are *either*, *neither*, *leisure*, *seize*, and *weird*.

Use *ei* after *c* or when the sound is not long *e*:

perceive	receiver	vein
conceited	deceit	eighth
ceiling	neighbor	weigh

The most common exceptions are *friend*, *mischief*, *handkerchief*, *sieve*, *view*, *fiery*, *financier*.

2 The term "spelling demons" is often used to refer to a group of common, useful words that are frequently misspelled. For some of the words it is mispronunciation that triggers the misspelling. For example, a person who pronounces the word *lightning* "lightening" is likely to put in an *e* in writing the word. If he pronounces *surprise* "suprise," he is likely to leave out the first *r*. Pronouncing words correctly can help eliminate many spelling errors.

But some words, even when they are pronounced correctly, cause trouble because their spelling does not match their pronunciation. For example, notice the silent *d*, *u*, and *p* in *handsome*, *guard*, and *raspberry*. And compare the difference between the spelling and the pronunciation of *sergeant*, *thorough*, and *Wednesday*. Some people have found that saying to themselves the "spelling pronunciation" of such a word— /wed nes dā/, for example—helps them spell the word correctly.

Here is a list of some of the most common spelling demons (divided into syllables to make their spelling easier to visualize). Look over the list to see how many of your personal spelling demons are on it.

ab sence	an a lyze
ac com mo date	an swer
ac quaint ance	anx ious
ac quire	arc tic
aisle	ath lete
a mong	ath let ic

bach e lor
bal ance
bar gain
bis cuit
bound ar y
bur eau
busi ness
cam paign
can di date
char ac ter is tic
chil dren
choc o late
choice
cho rus
colo nel
col umn
com mis sion
com mit tee
Con nect i cut
con science
cour te ous
cour te sy
crit i cism
debt
de ceased
de fense
de pend ent
did n't
dis as trous
dis eased
does n't
dou ble
drowned
em bar rassed
en trance
ex er cise
ex haust

ex ist ence
fas ten
Feb ru ar y
first
fo reign
for ty
gen u ine
ghost
gov ern ment
gram mar
guar an tee
guessed
hin drance
his tor y
hy giene
in tel li gent
in ter est ing
ir rel e vant
is land
jew el ry
judg ing
knew
knowl edge
lab o ra to ry
li brar y
li cense
lieu ten ant
ly ing
mar riage
meant
med i cine
mis cel la ne ous
mod ern
mort gage
mys ter i ous
ne ces si ty
nine teenth

nui sance

oc ca sion

of ten

o mis sion

op po site

pam phlet

par al lel

par lia ment

per haps

per ma nent

per spire

per suade

Phil ip pines

phys i cal

pic nick ing

plaque

pleas ant

pos si bly

prair ie

pre scrip tion

prob a bly

pro nun ci a tion

psy chol o gy

quan ti ty

ques tion naire

qui et

rec og nize

rec om mend

re mem brance

res taur ant

rhyme

rhythm

sand wich

scis sors

sense

sep a rate

sim i lar

sol dier

sol emn

sol u ble

soph o more

spon sor

straight

strength

stretch

sub tle

tech nique

ten den cy

to mor row

to ward

trag e dy

treas ur er

un con scious

un til

vac u um

vi o lence

weath er

wel come

which

wool en

3 *Homonyms* — word pairs like *fair* and *fare*, *its* and *it's*, *there* and *their* — are demons of another sort. It is not that people do not know the difference in spelling and meaning between such pairs. But when someone is concentrating on getting his ideas down on paper, he cannot (and should not) also be thinking about the spelling of each word he uses. It will sometimes happen, then, that he will write *"Their* was no answer" instead of *"There* was no answer." But though such a slip is natural, it should not go uncorrected.

By carefully proofreading, you can find and eliminate any such slips in your written work. Here are some common troublesome homonyms to watch for:

alter a coat	build an *altar*
baring his teeth	*bearing* a burden
reserved an upper *berth*	his daughter's *birth*
a *bough* of a tree	the *bow* of a ship
released the *brake*	*break* a window
her *bridal* gown	on the *bridle* path
a *canvas* knapsack	a house-to-house *canvass*
added some *coarse* sand	a *course* in electronics
a predicate *complement*	paid her a *compliment*
an apple *core*	a *corps* of doctors
a member of the *council*	the defense *counsel*
desert a friend	cherry pie for *dessert*
a car with *dual* controls	fought a *duel*
a *fair* day for the *fair*	borrowed bus *fare*
hit a *foul* ball	used to raise *fowl*
close the *gate*	slowed his *gait*
the fire in the *grate*	a *great* actor
didn't *hear* the bell	came *here* to live
heir to a fortune	polluting the *air*
a *hoarse* voice	riding a *horse*
wasted time in *idle* talk	worshiped an *idol*
robbed *its* nest	because *it's* late
left the *key* in the door	boats along the *quay*
a *lead* coin	*led* the parade
load the ships	a *lode* of copper
leaned against the *mantel*	a *mantle* of snow
a *metal* pipe	tested his *mettle*
a guided *missile*	read from the *missal*
peace and quiet	a *piece* of paper
landed the *plane*	rode across the *plain*

204

met with the *principal*   a *principle* of conduct
made a small *profit*   a *prophet* of doom
a driving *rain*   during Queen Anne's *reign*
a *stationary* crane   wrote on pink *stationery*
They're still *there.*   Is that *their* fault?
threw the ball to Al   crawled *through* the hole
too hot *to* drink   *two* tickets *to* the circus
Who's on first base?   *Whose* bat is that?

4 A small number of words have more than one acceptable spelling. Here are some examples of words with "variant" spellings:

adviser, advisor	hair's-breadth, hairsbreadth, hairbreadth
airplane, aeroplane	
bandanna, bandana	hiccup, hiccough
bronco, broncho	judgment, judgement
calorie, calory	license, licence
curtsy, curtsey	medieval, mediaeval
czar, tsar, tzar	millionaire, millionnaire
dialogue, dialog	mustache, moustache
dietitian, dietician	omelet, omelette
dryly, drily	raccoon, racoon
duffel, duffle	rumba, rhumba
enroll, enrol	sizable, sizeable
fiord, fjord	smolder, smoulder
gabardine, gaberdine	tepee, teepee
gasoline, gasolene	tornadoes, tornados
gypsy, gipsy	yodel, yodle

Most recent school and college dictionaries enter variant spellings. They also generally label spellings that are used chiefly in Britain. For instance, the British use an *-our* ending for words like *color* and *labor* (*colour, labour*). They spell words like *center* and *meter* with an *-re* instead of an *-er*, and *apologize* and *realize* with an *-ise*. They use an *x* in words like *connection* and *inflection* (*connexion, inflexion*). And they double more letters than we do, like the *g* of *wagon* (*waggon*), the *l* of *traveler* (*traveller*), and the *s* of *focused* (*focussed*).

In writing intended for an American audience American spellings are generally preferable. British spellings can be distracting to readers, especially readers unfamiliar with them. Otherwise you should feel free to use the spelling you prefer—so long as it is an accepted variant. But once you have made a choice, stick to it. Do not change from one spelling to another within the same piece of writing.

FILE VI: PRACTICE 1. *Decide which words in each of the following sentences should be capitalized. Copy the sentences on a sheet of paper, supplying the necessary capital letters. The figure in parentheses after each sentence shows how many capitals you will need to supply.*

1. About a half block south of the texaco station is an old quaker meeting house. (2)
2. The kimberly-clark corporation makes a number of paper products, including kleenex tissues. (4)
3. One of my mother's favorite books is rölvaag's *giants in the earth*, a novel about the norwegian immigrants in the dakotas. (5)
4. The best boston cream pie I have ever tasted is aunt edna's. (3)
5. Although stephen foster spent most of his life in the north, many of his best-known songs are about the south. (4)
6. We saw a number of michelangelo's sculptures in the medici chapel of san lorenzo church in florence. (7)
7. My uncle was born on the isle of man, near scotland, but he has lived in new york city almost all his life. (6)

8. Last year we spent twenty days on the *delta queen*, an air-conditioned steamship that followed the mississippi river to new orleans. (6)

9. In 1962, when he was eighty-six, thomas storke won the pulitzer prize for his editorial about the john birch society. (7)

10. Our exchange student from jordan finds geometry and chemistry 2 easy, but english and social studies hard. (3)

11. The captain and coach johnson both looked worried. (2)

12. What do you think of wilson high's chances, coach? (3)

13. The war between the virginia settlers and chief powhatan's tribes ended in an indian defeat. (4)

14. My cousin's father has a new ford convertible, but he used to drive a rambler station wagon. (2)

15. Vic sent in two wheaties box tops and got a set of colored pictures of north american birds. (3)

16. From the top of the hilton hotel you can see across town to stevenson high school, juneau hospital, and the carlson building. (9)

17. This year the kiwanis club held their bazaar on labor day in the grace church parking lot on the west side of town. (6)

18. Then little peter asked, "what should I get dad for his birthday, mom?" (4)

19. The jewish holiday of rosh hashanah doesn't come in spring; it comes in autumn, usually in september. (4)

20. Later major litvak told my grandfather that he was the author of "it's fun to be boss." (6)

FILE VI: PRACTICE 2.   *On a sheet of paper, write the plural forms of the following nouns, referring to a dictionary if necessary. Be ready to write the plurals from dictation of the singulars.*

1. cabbage
2. kohlrabi
3. onion
4. pimento
5. potato
6. radish
7. squash
8. tomato

9.	avocado	35.	sheep
10.	banana	36.	clematis
11.	strawberry	37.	crocus
12.	peach	38.	daisy
13.	pistachio	39.	jack-in-the-pulpit
14.	tangelo	40.	lily of the valley
15.	[Frank] Barnes	41.	trillium
16.	district attorney	42.	auditorium
17.	[John] Drury	43.	dormitory
18.	fishwife	44.	hutch
19.	gypsy	45.	pigsty
20.	hanger-on	46.	rotunda
21.	[Mike] Higgins	47.	shanty
22.	hillbilly	48.	studio
23.	ignoramus	49.	amethyst
24.	laundress	50.	ruby
25.	minuteman	51.	solitaire
26.	Nancy	52.	tiara
27.	son-in-law	53.	topaz
28.	two-year-old	54.	turquoise
29.	[Al] Voltz	55.	coat of mail
30.	anchovy	56.	derby
31.	dingo	57.	jersey
32.	donkey	58.	sombrero
33.	palomino	59.	turtleneck
34.	pony	60.	tuxedo

FILE VI: PRACTICE 3.   *On a sheet of paper, write the singular forms of the following nouns, referring to a dictionary if necessary. Be ready to write the singulars from dictation of the plurals.*

1.	Adonises	6.	blondes
2.	alumni	7.	blonds
3.	bacteria	8.	brownies
4.	banditti	9.	Burmese
5.	beaux	10.	busybodies

11. chassis /shas'ēz/
12. cherubim
13. cilia
14. coups d'état
15. criteria
16. dice
17. employees
18. employes
19. Eskimo
20. faux pas /fō' päz'/
21. fiancées
22. grottoes
23. indices
24. lice
25. lire
26. messieurs
27. moose
28. noes
29. oases
30. opera
31. pence
32. phenomena
33. quizzes
34. radii
35. referenda
36. saleswomen
37. sanitaria
38. sanitariums
39. savings bonds
40. sheep

FILE VI: PRACTICE 4. *Decide what the possessive form of each noun in parentheses should be. Then write the noun phrases— with the correctly spelled possessives—on a sheet of paper, numbering as you go.*

1. the (*ladies*) petition
2. the (*gentlemen*) word
3. the (*actress*) lines
4. their (*child*) demands
5. the (*mice*) panic
6. Mr. (*Harris*) fault
7. the (*Harrises*) dreams
8. Charles (*Dickens*) lectures
9. her (*brother-in-law*) truck
10. the (*Attorney General*) reply
11. Jane (*Austen*) novels
12. the (*Austens*) front lawn
13. one (*week*) pay
14. the (*children*) fingerprints
15. the (*alumni*) contributions
16. (*nobody*) fault
17. the (*siren*) wail
18. the (*lady*) toe
19. her (*two-year-old*) crib
20. most (*people*) attitude
21. ten (*cents*) worth
22. (*everybody*) problems
23. your (*baby*) pacifier
24. the (*babies*) bibs
25. (*Mitch*) old jacket
26. the (*horse*) mane
27. the (*horses*) hoofs
28. the (*mummy*) curse
29. the (*mummies*) coffins
30. her (*sons-in-law*) shares

FILE VI: PRACTICE 5. *Following each sentence two pronunciations are given of the word that belongs in the spot indicated by the blank. Decide which pronunciation is the standard one. Be ready to read the sentences aloud, substituting for the blanks the correctly pronounced words. (You may have to refer to your dictionary.)*

1. We stay away from Demon Lake because so many people have _____ there.
   /dround/   /droun'did/
2. I went to a big-league game _____.
   /wunst/   /wuns/
3. Yes, she can drive, but does she have a driver's _____?
   /lī'sns/   /lī'sn/
4. On our trip to Mexico we used ten rolls of _____.
   /fil'um/   /film/
5. Laura's father is a _____ physicist.
   /nü'klē ər/   /nü'kyü lər/
6. "I just don't care for _____ art," he answered.
   /mod'rən/   /mod'ərn/
7. Martha's _____ was driving the car.
   /fē'än sā/   /fē'äns/
8. No, it wasn't a man-made material; it was _____ alligator.
   /jen'yü wīn/   /jen'yü ən/
9. For dessert, everyone ordered _____ because it cost the least.
   /shėr'bət/   /shėr'bėrt/
10. "But how does a copper bracelet help _____?" I asked.
    /är thėr ī'tis/   /är thrī'tis/
11. Clifford is fat, much too fat for his _____.
    /hīt/   /hīth/
12. Two of the partners have been _____.
    /in dīt'id/   /in dik'tid/
13. We ran into Charles Spevak in the lobby of the _____ last night.
    /thē ā'tər/   /thē'ə tər/
14. She has a _____ accent, and all the boys fell for her.
    /suꜰн'ərn/   /suꜰн'rən/

15. If he'd cut out the _____ words, he could get his message on a stamp.
    /sú pėr′flü əs/   /sú′pər flü′əs/
16. His face glistened with _____.
    /pėr′spə rā′shən/   /pres′pə rā′shən/
17. Uncle Andy, a star _____, distrusted anyone who didn't like _____.
    /ath′lēt/   /ath′ə lēt/   /ath let′iks/   /ath ə let′iks/
18. No, the Greenbergs live _____ the street from the Lees, in the back apartment.
    /ə krôs′/   /ə krôst′/
19. Her dress is very _____, but her shoes!
    /chik/   /shēk/
20. To tell the truth, I didn't have the _____ to complain.
    /strenth/   /strength/

FILE VI: PRACTICE 6. *Be ready to read aloud the words in the following pairs, using the pronunciation key on page 188 if you need help with any of the symbols.*

1. bā′ғHerz
   bath′hou′ziz
2. bē′ting
   bet′ing
3. bib′lə kəl
   bī′sik′əl
4. sham pān′
   cham′pē ən
5. dē′snt
   di send′
6. ėr′nist
   ėr′ningz
7. fėr′ē
   fyu̇r′ē
8. hā′lō
   he lō′
9. hun′ē bē′
   hun′ē mün′
10. lôn′drē
    lôn′dər
11. māk
    mach
12. pėr′kē
    pes′kē
13. fāz
    frāz
14. shēth
    shēғн
15. stach′ü er′ē
    stach′ü esk′
16. tek′nə kal′ə tē
    tek′nə kul′ər

211

17. vā kā'shən
    vak'sə nāt
18. ven'is
    ven'ə zən

19. vij'ə lənt
    vij'ə lan'tē
20. hwis'kərd
    hwis'əld

FILE VI: PRACTICE 7. *In each of the following sentences commas are needed to separate items in a series. On a sheet of paper, write the number of each sentence. After it, write each word that should be followed by a comma, putting the comma after each. Be ready to read the sentences aloud, showing by your voice the spots where the commas belong.*

1. Our new swimming coach is short fat and bald.
2. During the summer I was expected to mow the lawn trim the hedge and weed the garden.
3. Don measured the fish shook his head in disbelief and then measured once again.
4. The firm now has branch offices in Rome Barcelona Paris Zurich and Berlin.
5. For breakfast we could order ham and eggs waffles and sausages or pancakes and maple syrup.
6. A week after Easter we were still finding eggs under the chairs behind the sofa in the closets and on the window sills.
7. Be sure to specify how many we need what price we are willing to pay and when we want them delivered.
8. Names like *Smith Butcher Carpenter Mason Miller* and *Weaver* were derived from the trade of a person.
9. Tom Dave and I finally learned that the way to become a good reader is to read and read and read.
10. On the first day of our trip we had breakfast in Illinois lunch in Indiana and dinner in Ohio.
11. Timmy can't decide whether to be a secret agent a nuclear physicist a detective or a fat-cat millionaire.
12. One of the coins slipped from his hand rolled down the steps and disappeared from sight.

13. Miss Breton speaks French Italian and Spanish fluently.
14. The manager hurried over to our table apologized for the waiter's clumsiness and offered to pay for having my suit cleaned.
15. At the first sign of spring he starts bringing home frogs toads turtles beetles and worms.
16. The crane swung out of control bumped into a concrete mixer and knocked over the foreman's shack.
17. Peter gave Grandma a vase Grandpa a pipe and me two tickets to the football game.
18. The bandstand was decorated with red white and blue pompons.
19. Every morning before school Cal has to make his bed wash the breakfast dishes and feed Smokey.
20. I wonder who he really is what he really wants and what he really writes in that little notebook he always carries.

FILE VI: PRACTICE 8. *In each of the following compound sentences a comma is needed to separate the main clauses joined by a coordinating conjunction. On a sheet of paper, write the number of each sentence. After it, write (1) the last word of the first clause, (2) the comma, (3) the conjunction. Be ready to read the sentences aloud, showing by your voice where the first clause ends and the second begins.*

1. Mrs. Solano had made costumes for everyone but Martin had grown too fat for his.
2. Everyone was urged to vote for the referendum was of special importance to our town.
3. Norma wrote a long letter to Sue and Ted and Ken added a few words in that illegible writing of his.
4. She offered to send a copy of the report to every member of the committee but the chairman told her not to bother.
5. They haven't heard the final score yet they're sure we won.
6. The next day Pete and I took turns driving the tractor for Dad couldn't raise his arm more than a few inches.

7. Corky walked over to the ladder and looked up and down on his head splashed the pailful of dirty water.
8. It was lucky for us that we didn't meet Larry or Bob would have started a fight then and there.
9. You ought to call him now and then you won't have to this evening.
10. The girls decided to ride home with Phil and Rudy and I were left waiting at the el stop.
11. We had to run for the bus was just rounding the corner.
12. The girls decided to ride home with Phil and Rudy and I was left waiting at the el stop.
13. You had better not tell Grace or her brothers will worm the secret out of her.
14. I like English and Spanish isn't too bad.
15. On the way home we met Nora and Joan and offered them our tickets but they had already seen the play.
16. Alicia dieted for a month and didn't lose an ounce so she stopped dieting.
17. Jerry can't work with gloves on and I can't work without them.
18. Kay and Roy broke up on Wednesday and on Thursday they started dating again.
19. Rob tensed his muscles and arched his back but still he couldn't lift the bar.
20. Jerry put a dime in and out came three packs of Juicy Fruit gum.

FILE VI: PRACTICE 9. *In each of the following sentences there is a parenthetical expression that should be set off. On a sheet of paper, write the number of each sentence. After it, write the parenthetical expression, placing a comma before and/or after it, as the sentence requires. Be ready to read the sentences aloud, showing by your voice the spots where the commas belong.*

1. Jennie for example would make an excellent general.
2. After all we can't be held responsible for his actions.

3. In some parts of the West Indies however laborers still carry heavy loads on their heads.
4. He managed to get around that corner without skidding believe it or not.
5. She is in fact an only child.
6. By the way where were you last Thursday evening from 7 to 10:30?
7. Mr. Benedict I noticed was sound asleep by the end of the first number.
8. But Robin Hood is just a *legendary* hero as you must know.
9. The librarian had it seems locked up all the Zane Grey books.
10. Mr. Brewster remember can't stand any kind of noise.
11. I simply think that you at least should have known better.
12. The average housewife on the other hand seems to enjoy soap operas.
13. That boyfriend of hers can be pretty annoying you must admit.
14. Moreover Ken is not above cheating now and then.
15. No one is perfect I'm afraid.
16. The Andersons own the swimming pool don't forget.
17. Ben Kiltze is without a doubt the stingiest man in Crandall County.
18. You can't expect to win them all you know.
19. To begin with sailing on Lake Michigan is not a sport for anyone who doesn't swim.
20. The children thank goodness were safe.

FILE VI: PRACTICE 10. *In each of the following sentences commas are needed to set off nouns of address and items in dates and addresses. On a sheet of paper, copy the sentences, putting in the needed commas. Be ready to read the sentences aloud, showing by your voice the spots where the commas belong.*

1. Have you noticed Ralph how many commercials they run in a single break?

2. Clifford was born on February 29 1960 and usually cele-brates his birthday on February 28 *and* March 1.

3. On May 13 1971 Edith Irving opened an account in a Swiss bank in the name of H. R. Hughes.

4. The doctor of today ladies and gentlemen does not rely on the word *abracadabra.*

5. Marie Andrew was just here with his mother.

6. Do you know that the roof is leaking Mr. Willis?

7. Mrs. Turco told us to write to the Bahama Islands Tourist Office 200 Southeast First Street Miami Florida 33130 for brochures to help us plan our trip.

8. Jerry was born on Friday September 13 1968 and his brother on Friday November 13 1970.

9. The letter was sent to Quincy Massachusetts but the Ho-gans live in Quincy Illinois.

10. Next week we'll take up high diving girls.

11. Don't forget Jim to turn off the TV before you leave.

12. Why don't you buy a program of your own you miser?

13. The phone book listed one J. E. Meinsen at 4625 Laurel Avenue Glenview and another at 77 Lakewood Place High-land Park.

14. That's wet paint you're sitting on Jerry.

15. Before the days of Zip Codes many letters intended for Watertown Mass. were sent to Watertown N.Y. by mistake.

16. On February 1 1972 Congresswoman Shirley Chisholm formally announced that she would seek the Presidential nomination.

17. Try to remember George to have the oil checked.

18. What she needs is a coat that really fits her Dad.

19. The corsages were ordered from Tallman's Flower Shop 3323 Roosevelt Road Kenosha Wisconsin 53140.

20. Just be thankful young lady that it was the car and not you that got hurt.

FILE VI: PRACTICE 11. *In each of the following sentences commas are needed to set off one or two appositives. On a sheet of paper, write the number of each sentence. After it, write each appositive (with its modifiers), placing a comma before and/or after it, as the sentence requires. Be ready to read the sentences aloud, showing by your voice the spots where the commas belong.*

1. The price twenty-six dollars seemed to me high for everyday shoes.
2. Phil is planning to play a duet with Patrick Henry's brother.
3. Jim Pierce the captain of the Bombers got into a bitter argument with the umpire a tough and rather stubborn old man and was thrown out of the game.
4. Mr. Flint the assistant director of the research group at the plant always wore his hat in his office.
5. The only clock in the cottage a battered Big Ben without a minute hand proved more confusing than helpful.
6. Celluloid the first of the modern plastics was invented by John Wesley Hyatt in 1869.
7. Harold soon realized that the next step doing the research for the paper would take more time than he had planned.
8. Mary Webster the tallest girl in the class had the part of the gnome.
9. My first suggestion to take the two cats with us was quickly vetoed by Dad.
10. Oswald's present a large bunch of plastic peonies was hardly the right thing for Miss Clayton.
11. Our gossipy next-door neighbor told us that Mrs. Green had hired Albert Schwartz a ten-year-old to baby-sit with Herkie her nine-year-old son.
12. The twins' room a counterpart of the Collier brothers' living room was a real challenge to the new housekeeper.
13. Peg had forgotten to add the sugar the most important of the ingredients.
14. We agreed to meet at Kremer's the drugstore across the street from the lawyer's office.
15. The Milwaukee zoo without a doubt one of the finest in the Midwest is on the must list for all our tourist friends.

16. The new owner a stern-looking man in his sixties wouldn't let us browse through the movie magazines.
17. Everyone thought that Uncle Cosmo a Victorian stick-in-the-mud would walk out during the second act.
18. Mr. Ventura offered Peter seventy-five dollars a week an unheard-of salary in those days.
19. The first important clue to the robber's identity a matchbook with an address scrawled inside was found by Mrs. Petri the cleaning woman.
20. Just then Frank Dutton cruised by in his dad's new car a dazzling Buick Skylark.

FILE VI: PRACTICE 12. *Read the following sentences and decide where commas are needed to set off introductory adverb clauses and verbal phrases. On a sheet of paper, write the number of each sentence. After it, write the last word of the introductory clause or phrase, following it with a comma. Be ready to read the sentences aloud, showing by your voice the spots where the commas belong.*

1. After Ozzie left the house seemed strangely quiet.
2. While Walter Cronkite was broadcasting a news item was handed to him.
3. Not wanting Dino to suspect Arnold changed the subject.
4. "And when you have finished Dad's shirts need ironing," said Mother.
5. When I walked through the classrooms were deserted.
6. Mistaking him for my cousin Don rushed up and slapped him on the back.
7. Before you go see Mrs. Fowler.
8. As soon as the pond freezes Harry is going to get a hockey team together.
9. Hoping to impress her Uncle Leo ordered raw oysters.
10. Since you'll probably see Andrew before I will tell him I have the four tickets for the game.
11. Holding his breath Winthrop handed his report card to his father.

12. To make them produce more hens have been provided with everything from special vitamins to stereophonic music.
13. When Claude comes to bat the left fielder automatically moves back.
14. While we watched the mouse carried its five baby mice to safety.
15. Being a snoop Donald read the note before passing it on to Bernadette.
16. Because the tunes were pleasing and simple people remembered them.
17. To commemorate the victory the Romans constructed a triumphal arch.
18. After eating the banana split Swede ordered a pineapple soda.
19. If you expect your dog to obey you must train him.
20. While in the bank cashing the check Mother witnessed a holdup.

FILE VI: PRACTICE 13. *In the following sentences the adjective clauses are italicized. Decide which of the clauses are nonrestrictive and should be set off by commas. On a sheet of paper, write the number of each sentence. After it, write each nonrestrictive clause, placing a comma before and/or after it, as the sentence requires. (After the number of any sentence without a nonrestrictive clause, write "None.") Be ready to read the sentences aloud, showing by your voice the spots where the commas belong.*

1. Old Mrs. Watson *who never forgot a face* was sure that the Frank Maxwell *who was selling the stock* was the Frank Maxwell *who had swindled her husband.*
2. In 1803 Napoleon *who needed money for his military campaigns* sold the Louisiana Territory to the United States.
3. By Easter Sunday the tulips *which Dad and I planted last fall* will be in full bloom.
4. Nothing is more annoying than a train announcer *who mumbles his words.*

5. At this point Ann's cousin Clayton *who is usually quite cowardly* showed a most remarkable courage.

6. The Europeans learned to play chess from the Arabs *who had, in their turn, learned the game from the Persians.*

7. My part *which was simply to moan and groan and rattle some heavy chains off stage* was not as easy as you might think.

8. By the way, the waiter *who was insolent to Mrs. Vanderpool Friday* is looking for a new job.

9. Gary made some fishhooks from the ribs of Mr. Kusick's old black umbrella *which Mrs. Kusick had discarded.*

10. Helen told us that Mick Clooney *who was bored with just being one fourth of a quartet* started working on a combination song and comedy act of his own.

11. Uncle Cy *who felt completely out of place in such la-di-da company* was happy that nobody paid much attention to him.

12. Yesterday a junior from our school and a senior from Wilson High competed in the tennis finals. The junior *who had a better serve* won.

13. Al's forehead *which had been protected from the sun by a straw hat* contrasted sharply with the rest of his face *which was deeply tanned and windburned.*

14. Last night at dinner Gloria told us that Leo Martin *whose girl friend was the chairman of the reception committee* was the only fellow *who showed up at the Women's Lib tea.*

15. Mother's only uncle *whom we hadn't seen or heard from for years* left us his summer cottage in his will.

16. Marilyn finally got a seat next to a man *who was wearing greasy overalls and a filthy cap.*

17. Cy had only one pair of shoes *which he wore for school and for play and for Sunday best.*

18. Adria *whose mother is a book reviewer for our local paper* is always lending me books by authors *who are much too deep for me.*

19. A couple of hours later we went back to check on Bobby *who was patiently fishing in the same spot.*

20. Eileen was wearing her sister's new silver pumps *which were a size too short for her.*

FILE VI: PRACTICE 14.   *In the following sentences the participial phrases are italicized. Decide which of the phrases are nonrestrictive and should be set off by commas. On a sheet of paper, write the number of each sentence. After it, write each nonrestrictive phrase, placing a comma before and/or after it, as the sentence requires. (After the number of any sentence without a nonrestrictive phrase, write "None.") Be ready to read the sentences aloud, showing by your voice the spots where the commas belong.*

1. *Suspecting a trap* Mannix moved cautiously.
2. Grandfather Curtis *moving quickly for a man of his age* bounded off the porch two steps at a time.
3. A car *skidding on wet pavement* is a terrifying sight.
4. Henry stood beside me throughout the performance *making silly wisecracks the whole time.*
5. Margo bought two Indonesian fans at the bazaar. The one *made of buffalo hide* was ornately decorated; the other one *carved from sandalwood* was plainer.
6. The Saint Bernard *having a wonderful sense of smell* can find persons *buried several feet under the snow.*
7. The policeman *directing the traffic at that corner* has a hard job.
8. The boy on top *hearing his mother's stern command to stop* reluctantly let go of his opponent's hair.
9. Few of the diners even noticed the two men *seated at the table in the corner.* The one *wearing dark glasses* was Bob Hope. His companion *busily taking notes on the back of an envelope* was a reporter.
10. Officer O'Keefe *directing the traffic at that corner* motioned us to go on.
11. Every member *missing three meetings* will be dropped from the club.
12. At the next stop a tall, good-looking boy and a pretty girl got on the bus. The boy *wearing a faded pair of blue jeans* was on his way to the Jensen orchards.
13. Alfred could not decide whether to buy the corduroy car coat or the brown and beige plaid suit. He really needed a

new suit; but the coat *lined with a bright red fleece* would impress the fellows more.

14. Mr. Corbett absent-mindedly left the train without his umbrella and the brown leather briefcase he always carried. The briefcase *containing some top-secret documents* mysteriously disappeared before the train reached Chicago.

15. The next minute the cigar exploded *startling Uncle Dino out of his wits.*

16. *Reminded of his promise to take us bowling* Dad just grinned.

17. A man *standing beside the bridge* flagged us to a stop. Grandpa pulled over and got out of the car *grumbling at the delay.*

18. Dennis *almost bursting with pride* held up his trophy for everyone to see.

19. *Not wanting to wake Mom and Dad* I took off my shoes and tiptoed upstairs.

20. Sergeant Ashby shadowed the men for three days *hoping to discover Turek's hideout.*

FILE VI: PRACTICE 15. *In each of the following sentences a comma is needed for clearness. On a sheet of paper, write the number of each sentence. After it, write the word that should be followed by a comma. Be ready to read each sentence aloud, showing by your voice the spot where the comma belongs.*

1. In our class of thirty six speak Spanish at home.
2. The year before he had given up his job to go back to college.
3. Next June Helen and Alice are going to Lily Lake for a few days.
4. Tom waited for his sister to walk in and out the back door he ran.
5. In comparison with these salary increases mean nothing.
6. For a person who really likes to hike twenty miles a day is not too much.
7. But in the period we are concerned with few people had telephones.

8. Inside the house was spotless and quite attractive.
9. Those who left left during the second intermission.
10. I would sand the table top now and then paint it.
11. Just a minute before the squad car had cruised past his house.
12. During the winter time dragged more slowly than ever for Elizabeth.
13. At our school dances are held in the girls' gym.
14. To Steve Allen was the man to beat in the primary.
15. Ever since Larry has counted to ten before going off half-cocked.
16. Why don't we eat now and then go to the movie?
17. On weekends only members are permitted to play tennis here at the club.
18. To the officer who won the promotion meant a chance to reorganize the department.
19. According to Joe Mannix is the most believable of the private eyes.
20. In spite of this defeat seemed inevitable.

FILE VI: PRACTICE 16. *Read the following sentences and decide where semicolons are needed to separate the two parts of a compound sentence or the items in a series in which the items contain commas. Decide also where commas are needed—for nonrestrictive modifiers, nouns of address, items in series, items in addresses, etc. On a sheet of paper, copy the sentences, putting in the needed punctuation. Be ready to read the sentences aloud, showing by your voice the spots where the semicolons and commas belong.*

1. Mr. Oswald was once an intrepid mountain climber now he hates to walk from the kitchen to his room upstairs.
2. Small batches of these counterfeit bills were passed in San Mateo California in Valmora New Mexico and in Shopton Iowa.
3. Two of the fellows had to leave early they have after-school jobs at Carson's.

4. My dad is a soft-spoken Democrat my mother is an outspoken Republican.

5. Mrs. Farley keeps in touch with pen pals in Birmingham England Beirut Lebanon and Wellington New Zealand.

6. Nancy wasn't interested in our plans she had other things to do.

7. The most exciting episodes in his life were his escape from the prison fortress his bold unrelenting pursuit of Colvin who had planted the evidence against him and his winning the hand of Aurora the proud and beautiful Princess of Ardennes.

8. At first Fitz agreed to sell me his old motorcycle later he tried to wriggle out of the bargain.

9. Uncle Gene liked the new Gremlins best in fact he ordered one.

10. The boys waited until Mr. Reilly turned his back then they sneaked out.

11. The office manager wouldn't listen to reason he fired both of us on the spot.

12. The three main characters are Darrel Fenwick a hard-boiled newspaper reporter Felicia Harris an advertising-agency executive who was once jilted by Fenwick and Joseph Josephs whose fantastic money-making schemes serve to bring the two of them together again.

13. Marie is going to ask her father to plan the banquet menu for us he is a chef at La Rondelle.

14. In the three years Mr. Martin was president the company opened branch offices in Quincy Illinois Oshkosh Wisconsin Ann Arbor Michigan and Silver Spring Maryland.

15. Uncle Abner had left twenty thousand dollars to his sister Amy who had brought him up twenty thousand dollars to the Kenton Halfway House which he had been instrumental in founding and a single dollar to his son Leroy who had angered him by becoming a circus clown.

16. To the wealthy he promised tax cuts to the poor he promised added benefits under social security increased unemployment compensation and a higher minimum wage.

17. Don't move George there's a hornet on your collar.
18. The acting was excellent the script was pure soap opera.
19. Our history teacher is never satisfied with fine-sounding generalizations she insists on our backing up our statements with concrete evidence.
20. One fellow filled the gas tank another cleaned the windshield.

FILE VI: PRACTICE 17. *Read the following sentences and decide where colons are needed (to introduce a formal quotation or appositives at the end of a sentence) and where underlining should be used (for titles and for words or letters used as words). Decide also where commas, question marks, and quotation marks are needed. On a sheet of paper, copy the sentences, putting in the necessary punctuation. Be ready to read the sentences aloud, making the intended meaning clear by pauses and changes in your voice.*

1. Mr. Williams ended his address with a proverb from Poor Richard's Almanac He that is of the opinion that money will do everything may well be suspected of doing everything for money.
2. All objects have two forms of inertia the inertia of rest and the inertia of motion.
3. The firm has representatives in the following European cities Milan Geneva Granada Essen and Lille.
4. Is this this an adjective or a pronoun he asked pointing to the first word in the title This Is Your Life.
5. My sister thought that Bette looked more chic than Betty so she always spelled her name with a final e and no y.
6. The box-office favorites in this state were the following Nicholas and Alexandra Fiddler on the Roof and The Hospital.
7. In the last chapter of his book How Children Fail John Holt presents this thought-provoking statement The true test of intelligence is not how much we know how to do but how we behave when we don't know what to do.

8. After paying tribute to all the employees the publisher gave special credit to the following the sports editor the layout director and the advertising manager.

9. Harry J. Skornia professor of radio and television at the University of Illinois clearly indicates the raison d'être of his book Television and the News by dedicating it in these words To the late Edward R. Murrow and the many fine and dedicated newsmen of America whose lot this book seeks to make easier so the people of America may be better informed.

10. Dickens has given the world many memorable characters Scrooge Mr. Micawber David Copperfield and Uriah Heep to mention only a few.

11. In her report she had spelled the playwright's name in three different ways Shakespear Shakspere and Shakespeare.

12. On the bronze plaque below the statue was engraved this sentence A truly great man will neither trample on a worm nor sneak to an emperor.

13. Anyone Grandfather Strom insisted could be an unqualified social success if he limited his conversation to two sentences It certainly is interesting and I do believe you're right.

14. Beverly Hillbillies and Green Acres doomed by TV critics to instantaneous failure quickly became national favorites.

15. Three newspapers were singled out for special acclaim the Wall Street Journal the Christian Science Monitor and the Times.

16. I would say their candidate has three strikes against him his total lack of experience his reluctance to face the issues squarely and his well-deserved reputation as a wheeler-dealer.

17. If for example you pronounce across with a final t you will probably misspell the word.

18. Hospital officials issued the following statement The governor is out of danger now and signs are good for a speedy recovery.

19. The typist had reversed the e and the r in modern and the boss hadn't noticed it.
20. Six American authors have won the Nobel Prize for literature Sinclair Lewis Eugene O'Neill Pearl Buck William Faulkner Ernest Hemingway and John Steinbeck.

FILE VI: PRACTICE 18. *Read the following sentences and decide where dashes are needed to indicate an abrupt change in the thought or to set off parenthetical comments, appositives, or nonrestrictive modifiers. Decide also what other marks are needed (commas, question marks, exclamation marks). On a sheet of paper, copy the sentences, putting in the necessary punctuation. Be ready to read the sentences aloud, making the intended meaning clear by appropriate pauses and changes in your voice.*

1. It took the serviceman only two minutes to discover the cause of the trouble an empty gas tank!
2. Every Wednesday afternoon the barbershops in Elm Grove close at twelve on Wednesdays Joe Parola went to the beach to practice tumbling.
3. No sooner had he recovered from the accident than but that's another story.
4. Clem Stacey you remember him don't you made the touchdown.
5. Ben is the smartest boy in the school if you ask Ben.
6. The next day everything and I do mean everything went wrong.
7. Jeff's brother Tony he is the only serious one in that family is really worried about Jeff's skipping school.
8. Mike went off to the wrestling match with Ernie and I had to go to the play a dull boring senseless comedy.
9. Only three schools Bradford High Thomas More and St. Catherine's expressed any interest in our ideas for a Media Fair.
10. The greedy cod swallows practically anything leather rubber oil cans and even scissors.

11. Mayor Loosa what a fake he is is giving the keynote address tonight.
12. Only one person can stop forest fires you.
13. Clifford gave the bellhop a quarter that was all that was left of the twenty dollars and crossed the lobby to the house phones.
14. The leader of the pirates Sam Reindl played the part was a loud-mouthed monster with a long hooked nose and a black patch over one eye.
15. The next morning but why should I bore you with all these details?
16. Two weeks later the whole blessed family Uncle Pat Aunt Kay Ellen and Ian were still at our cottage and showed no signs of ever leaving.
17. It took Mr. Billings an hour to get to the important point how much I would be paid.
18. Right then Howard and Grace came by and no that happened later.
19. This strange diet two large perchlike fish a shark a bird and two coconuts kept the three men on the raft alive for more than a month.
20. In the seventeenth century Salé it rhymes with *café* was one of the active pirate centers in North Africa.

FILE VI: PRACTICE 19. *In each of the following sentences parentheses are needed to enclose a tucked-in explanation or numbers or letters used to mark the items in a series. Some of the sentences also need commas (to separate items in a series, to separate main clauses, to set off parenthetical expressions, etc.). On a sheet of paper, copy the sentences, putting in the necessary punctuation. Be ready to read the sentences aloud, making the intended meaning clear by pauses and changes in your voice.*

1. Walking from our apartment to the Mastersons' apartment a distance of only eight blocks we passed at least ten antique shops.

2. Most of the letters come from a townspeople who have complaints about the local government b reformers who enjoy airing their views and c people who want to see their names in print.
3. Ed Farrell Laura Geist and Steve Ellis all of them seniors were in charge of the Science Fair.
4. Cliff was born on February 29 it was a leap year of course and on March 1 his grandfather opened a Golden Eagle bank account for him.
5. Mr. Throwdon contributed just a thousand dollars a trifling sum of course for a millionaire but he promised to double whatever amount the parishioners collected.
6. We cannot continue publishing the school paper unless 1 we raise the subscription rate 2 we sell more ads and 3 we use a much cheaper paper.
7. The sausage weighed two kilos almost four and a half pounds and that added to everything else made my knapsack pretty heavy.
8. Senator Adlai Stevenson the son of a two-time Presidential nominee was asked if he would be a candidate for the Presidency.
9. The bill for the car repairs was eighteen pounds that would be forty-three dollars or so in our money so we went without lunch the rest of the week.
10. Everyone says that the new principal Mr. Theisen retired last June is quite a disciplinarian.
11. Monaco is tiny its area no more than half a square mile but it is well known because of two special attractions Monte Carlo and Princess Grace.
12. We made the trip from Rome to Borbona in less than two hours on Dino's Vespa as lively as its name *Wasp* suggests.

FILE VI: PRACTICE 20. *Some of the following numbered items consist of one sentence; others consist of more than one. Copy the items, adding quotation marks and capital letters and all other punctuation that is needed. Be ready to read the sentences aloud, showing by your voice which parts are direct quotations and which are simply explanatory.*

1. Are you serious Matt asked do you really mean it
2. Watch out Dad shouted don't you see that car
3. Did you notice whispered Angela on the way out how many times Mr. Blivens said life is what you make it
4. Are we supposed to read To Build a Fire or The Madness of John Harned or both he asked
5. The projector continued Mr. Paxton is not to be used without permission from the librarian
6. Oh I know which one is the shortstop the girl cooed but where are the linebackers
7. Father Malone replied that's all foolishness my boy in spite of its pleasant sound
8. Getting that gang to cooperate groaned Mike would be a minor miracle everyone wants to be the boss
9. Paint me as I am said Cromwell to Peter Lely the portrait painter if you leave out the scars and wrinkles I will not pay you a shilling
10. Why aren't you laughing where's your sense of humor Dan asked
11. Well what would you do Leo asked if someone pointed a gun at you and said this is a holdup
12. Ann will be there Mrs. Penn said even if she has to walk
13. The conductor scowled at me and said you're too big to ride on a half-fare ticket
14. Who broke my basement window asked Mr. Hull angrily
15. What do you want to eat the waitress asked wiping off the counter in front of me
16. Ted and Alice want to go bowling Bernie explained but we'd rather go to the zoo
17. What are you looking for now inquired Gloria
18. If you were my bowling shoes replied Bernie where would you be
19. Hello said a gruff voice let me speak with the principal

20. If you pay for my hamburger Ted went on I can go to the movies with you otherwise I won't have enough money for the show

FILE VI: PRACTICE 21. [*Note: All the practice drills in this section are set up as dictations in which the spelling words appear in sentences. Having to write the words in sentences rather than as isolated items in a list provides the student with an approximation of a real writing situation—in which his attention is focused on the meaning of the words he writes, not on their spelling. Thus the drills provide fairly reliable tests of the student's mastery of the spelling.*]

Be ready to write the following sentences from dictation:

DRILL A—doubling final consonants
1. The manager admitted that the robbery was regrettable.
2. The saddest occurrence was the dropping of the swimming classes as an economy measure.
3. Larry preferred to think that the biggest deterrent for the beginners was the fear of injury.
4. Dan dropped the suitcases, slammed through the gates, and hopped on the train just as it was pulling out.
5. It had never occurred to Mr. Stopper that the weeds could be controlled.
6. Helen has never regretted transferring to North High.
7. Aunt May grabbed little Timmy, dragged him to the kitchen, and scrubbed his face.
8. I had planned to use the biggish sheets of wrapping paper myself.

DRILL B—final silent *e*
1. Mom is still hoping that they will both be coming for Christmas.
2. Pat was in the dining room writing a report, while I was in the backyard spading and raking.
3. Shining that flashlight in his eyes was truly inexcusable, and forging his signature was wholly unforgivable.

4. I have been advising her that continuing the argument about her retirement would hardly be advantageous for her.
5. Earl has been hiring some mighty careless workers lately.
6. Nora kept right on bandaging his arm, not noticing that he was scarcely breathing.

DRILL C — words with *y*
1. Ella enjoys hurrying but is annoyed if anyone hurries her.
2. Sam worries most if he doesn't have any real worrying to do.
3. While we were carrying the heaviest loads, he was pitying us, which was the silliest thing he could do.
4. Luckily, Jim was busily studying when Dad finally found him.
5. The page walked happily toward the prettiest of the ladies and notified her that she would soon be marrying the king.
6. His greediness steadily grew, which easily explains his pitiful loneliness.

DRILL D — adding prefixes and suffixes
1. The dissatisfied tenants soon made their disapproval known.
2. It was quite unnatural for him to do any unnecessary work.
3. An unnamed terror stalked through the valley, unnerving all the villagers.
4. Actually, Paul's meanness is due to his deafness.
5. I misspelled a few words and he misprinted a few more, so the announcement was unreadable.
6. His wife's pleasantness and humanness partly make up for his stubbornness.
7. Clifford usually dresses sloppily, though he thinks of himself as really neat.
8. Since he is dishonest, disloyal, and disorderly, we are dissatisfied and would like to dissolve our partnership.
9. Having misread the directions, he misquoted them to us, and we ended by misleading others.

10. It was the suddenness of the attack rather than its fierceness that defeated them.

DRILL E — *ei* and *ie*
1. I believe the chief and his niece saw the thief take the gold piece.
2. Neither I nor my friends had a handkerchief to lend to our neighbor upstairs.
3. The chief gave a shriek, and the siege began.
4. This is the eighth time he has weighed that weird fish.
5. How is the view from the ceiling, friend?
6. His grievance is that the receiver wasn't there to catch his pass.
7. When Dr. Johnson perceived this deceit, he seized the financier.

DRILL F — spelling demons
1. In the absence of the colonel the lieutenant will answer all grammar questions.
2. The treasurer guessed that the genuine jewelry was hidden in the laboratory, didn't he?
3. An intelligent sponsor would probably have the good sense to analyze the prescription before he would recommend the medicine.
4. The question is which of the candidates has the physical strength to weather the campaign.
5. Perhaps he meant that a sophomore has a tendency to go straight to the point when trying to persuade others.
6. Judging by Jim's pronunciation of that double column of miscellaneous demons in the questionnaire, I would guarantee that there will be no criticism of his speeches in parliament.
7. On forty similar occasions his knowledge of subtle business techniques has helped him avoid disastrous violence and permanent tragedy.
8. It was characteristic that the picnicking children recognized the embarrassed ghost and made him feel welcome.

DRILL G—homonyms

1. The two men were too tired to load the metal pipes back on their truck.
2. After working all day in the rain, we looked forward to a fire in the grate, a great dessert after dinner, and an evening of peace and quiet.
3. As they walked along the quay, Mabel dropped the key, which bounced and then disappeared through a crack in a plank.
4. The defense counsel questioned him about the psychology course he had taken.
5. Above the mantel was a painting of Lady Ellen wearing a red velvet mantle.
6. Then a second voice, hoarse with fatigue, announced that the missile had hit its mark.
7. A canvass of the staff showed that no one in the diplomatic corps was ever idle, whether the weather was fair or foul.
8. Even a second-rate prophet could have told him that selling lead tokens for bus fares would bring very little profit.
9. Who's the movie idol whose picture is on every magazine cover these days?
10. It's part of his plan to see that they're caught with their hands in the till.

In this index, references to exercises are indicated by ✔.